Southeast Asia: A Very Short Introduction

VERY SHORT INTRODUCTIONS are for anyone wanting a stimulating and accessible way into a new subject. They are written by experts, and have been translated into more than 45 different languages.

The series began in 1995, and now covers a wide variety of topics in every discipline. The VSI library now contains over 500 volumes—a Very Short Introduction to everything from Psychology and Philosophy of Science to American History and Relativity—and continues to grow in every subject area.

Very Short Introductions available now:

Available soon:

For more information visit our website

www.oup.com/vsi/

James R. Rush

SOUTHEAST ASIA

A Very Short Introduction

OXFORD
UNIVERSITY PRESS

OXFORD

UNIVERSITY PRESS

Oxford University Press is a department of the University of Oxford.
It furthers the University's objective of excellence in research, scholarship,
and education by publishing worldwide. Oxford is a registered trademark of
Oxford University Press in the UK and certain other countries.

Published in the United States of America by Oxford University Press
198 Madison Avenue, New York, NY 10016, United States of America.

Library of Congress Cataloging-in-Publication Data
Names: Rush, James R. (James Robert), 1944- author.
Title: Southeast Asia : a very short introduction / James R. Rush.
Description: Oxford : Oxford University Press, [2018] |
Includes bibliographical references and index. |
Identifiers: LCCN 2017043737 (print) | LCCN 2017044526 (ebook) |
ISBN 9780190248772 (updf) | ISBN 9780190248789 (epub) |
ISBN 9780190248796 (online component) |
ISBN 9780190248765 | ISBN 9780190248765q (pbk. ;qalk. paper)
Subjects: LCSH: Southeast Asia.
Classification: LCC DS521 (ebook) | LCC DS521 .R87 2018 (print) |
DDC 959—dc23
LC record available at https://lccn.loc.gov/2017043737

Printed by Integrated Books International, United States of America
on acid-free paper

Contents

List of illustrations

Introduction

Southeast Asia is a region of vast complexity, and scholarship about it is equally vast and complex. This slender book draws upon a broad body of scholarship. Barely a sentence fails to reflect the ideas and scholarly writing of my mentors and colleagues and others from whom I have learned. Readers familiar with the literature will discern the footprints of Harry Benda, John Smail, O. W. Wolters, Benedict Anderson, Anthony Reid, James Scott, J. S. Furnivall, Thongchai Winichakul, and a host of others whose work has shaped the field.

This volume is a "very short introduction," and so it does not attempt to capture fully the deep research and nuanced arguments of this scholarship. Instead, its purpose is to tell a complicated story simply and legibly. Its historical arc focusing on kingdoms, colonies, and nations is deliberately formulaic, designed to provide a structured narrative around which otherwise random events and anecdotal information about Southeast Asia (or the day's news, for that matter) can be understood in the context of larger patterns of history, politics, and society. This narrative can be—indeed, it is meant to be—explored, elaborated, and critiqued through further study. The "Suggestions for Further Reading" at the back will get you started.

Southeast Asia: A Very Short Introduction is also intentionally colloquial. Terms are used such as trade hubs, traffic patterns, and mini-kings, for example, the latter to describe an array of persons who ruled over small territories (mini-kingdoms) throughout Southeast Asia under many different titles. Likewise, certain terms are employed that are often applied more narrowly in scholarship—mandala, for example—to describe general patterns applying to the region at large. Thongchai Winichakul's use of the term *geo-body*, to mean a modern border-bounded nation-state, is another example. The word *Native*, capitalized, is used here to convey the colonial-era practice of categorizing indigenous Southeast Asians officially (and subordinately) in the law.

Southeast Asia also prioritizes the familiar. East Timor will be East Timor, although it is officially known as Timor-Leste and also as Timor Lorosa'e. Burma will be Burma, except when referring to the contemporary state of Myanmar. Burmans will be Burmans, not Bama. And so on. The spellings of Southeast Asian names can vary considerably when rendered in English. I have followed familiar scholarly conventions.

One cannot possibly acknowledge everyone who has contributed to a general book like this one. But I am grateful to my undergraduate students at Arizona State University (ASU), in dialogue with whom the narrative of this book has evolved, and also to several former graduate students whose work has informed my work. These include Maria Ortuoste, Christopher Lundry, Duan Zhidan, Zhipei Chi, Sze Chieh Ng, and Alex Arifianto. Particular thanks go to William McDonald, an ASU student at Barrett, the Honors College, who worked diligently collecting data about the contemporary region. I am also indebted to my faculty colleagues in Southeast Asia studies at ASU from whom I am constantly learning. They include Sheldon Simon, Juliane Schober, Ted Solis, Karen Adams, Christopher Duncan (now at Rutgers), Leif Jonsson, James Eder, Mark Woodward, Pauline Cheong, Sarah Shair-Rosenfield, Peter Suwarno, Sina Machander, Le-Pham Thuy-Kim, and Ralph Gabbard. Finally, I want to express my gratitude and love to my wife, Sunny Benitez-Rush, who enriches everything I do, including this book.

Chapter 1
What is Southeast Asia?

Southeast Asia is a sprawling neighborhood of hot countries that straddles the equator. Its eleven nations lie between India and China and form the great tropical cusp of Asia. Here societies drawing from Buddhism, Hinduism, Islam, Christianity, and Confucianism (alongside myriad other traditions) have rubbed shoulders over centuries and created a vast profusion of distinctive yet ever-shifting cultures. It is among the most dynamic regions on earth.

Mainland Southeast Asia, the southern apron of the continent of East Asia, is home to hundreds of ethnic groups that are today the citizens of Myanmar, Thailand, Laos, Cambodia, and Vietnam. Island (or maritime) Southeast Asia includes the Malay Peninsula and two huge archipelagos whose even more diverse populations are now citizens of Indonesia, Malaysia, Singapore, Brunei, East Timor, and the Philippines. The entire region stretches some 3,000 miles from end to end and 2,500 miles north to south, an area larger than Europe. It contains 625 million people, around 9 percent of the world's population.

For the most part, Southeast Asia is verdant and wet, with rainfalls averaging 60 inches a year and, in many places, monsoon rains that arrive reliably each year to water the rice fields, vegetable gardens, and fruit trees that for centuries have sustained its rural villages. But here and there drier patches are found where rain is scarce. In eastern Indonesia people say that their arid islands are the dirt flicked from the fingernails of the Creator after he finished making the rest of the world.

Although Southeast Asia's complex wind, water, and elevation patterns have created multiple human habitats, scholars have found it useful to begin with two archetypal ones: hills and plains. Large expanses of the region rise above 1,000 feet. Until very recently, these hills and mountains have been a world apart, an alternative human habitat dominated by dense old-growth forests interlaced by free-flowing rivers and streams. In these vast and inaccessible uplands, farmers developed strategies for living sustainably by creating temporary hill farms amid the forest—by cutting down a patch of trees, burning the debris, and planting rice and other crops amid the charred remains. A hillside "swidden" like this could be bountiful for a year or two, after which the farmers moved on to another patch as the old one wooded over again and restored the forest.

Hill farms of this kind existed everywhere in Southeast Asia, enabling highly diverse customs and characterized by distinctive textiles, jewelry, tattoos, handcrafts, and spiritual practices. From Myanmar to the Philippines hundreds of such groups could be found. One may have heard of the Lisu, Mien, and Hmong of the Burma-Thai-Lao uplands, the Rhade and other Montagnards of Vietnam, the Iban of Malaysia and Indonesia, and the Ifugao and Mangyan of the Philippines. Hill peoples like these maintained a variety of contacts with their lowland neighbors, most especially an up-river and down-river exchange of forest products (rattan, damar, bird's nests) for lowland valuables such as heirloom porcelains and outboard motors. Otherwise, they remained aloof, clinging to the sanctuary provided by their inaccessible habitat.

These small populations of resilient, adaptable, and often-shifting hill folk built their longhouses and villages along the free-flowing mountain rivers that eventually flowed downward, aggregated with other branches, and formed the great tidal rivers of Southeast Asia's lowland plains.

Just as slash-and-burn farming became the dominant agricultural pattern of the hills, wet-rice farming dominated the plains. Instead of temporary swiddens, in the lowlands farmers created permanent, bunded fields designed to capture water and manage its depth as green rice plants sprouted, rose through the shallow waters of the artificial pond, and finally matured and yellowed as farmers drained the paddies to make dry fields at harvest time. For centuries past and until today, paddy fields have dominated the cultivated landscape of lowland Southeast Asia and supported its large sedentary populations, even as vast tracts of lowlands also remained forested until recent times.

Interspersed with vegetable gardens, fruit orchards, and lush groves of trees, this verdant lowland habitat has supported large populations of farmers as well as the region's major societies and states throughout history. It is the plains that host Southeast Asia's larger ethnic groups—the Burmans, Thai, Khmer, Vietnamese, Malay, Javanese, Filipino—as well as the greater concentrations of people adhering to major world religions. Most of Southeast Asia's Buddhists, Muslims, Christians, and Hindus are people of the plains. In short, almost always when we speak of Southeast Asia, we are speaking of the lowland societies of the plains.

Today, the old dichotomy of hills and plains is breaking down. Once a lightly populated region, Southeast Asia is now bursting with people. And they are changing its old landscapes— penetrating the hills to open giant mines and to harvest logs and palm oil; overtaking forests, vacant wetlands, and vast acres of village rice paddies to create a modern landscape of exploding megacities, sprawling suburbs, and burgeoning industrial zones; and blanketing great swaths of countryside with agribusiness

CONTEMPORARY SOUTHEAST ASIA AND ITS

1. Contemporary Southeast Asia and its nation-states

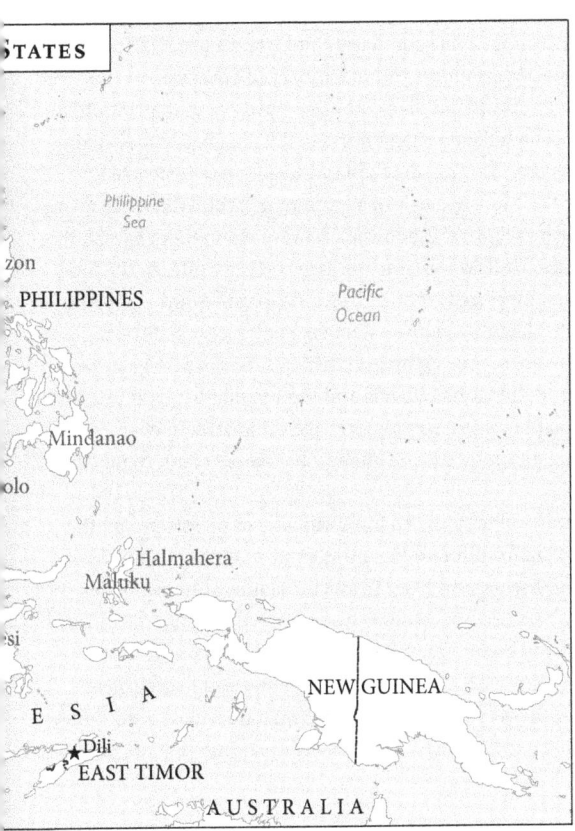

Philippine
Sea

zon

PHILIPPINES

Pacific
Ocean

Mindanao

olo

Halmahera
Maluku

si

E S I A

Dili
EAST TIMOR

NEW GUINEA

AUSTRALIA

plantations that produce bananas, coconuts, sugar, and rubber. Shrimp and fish farms now cover the region's coasts, which once were lined with mangroves.

In Southeast Asia today, no one is wholly off the grid. Even the most remote mountain sanctuaries and islands are within reach of the capital, technology, and machinery of government that are pulling every group and place into the matrix of globalization. For the Iban of the hills of central Borneo, it is logging and oil-palm plantations. For the Ifugao of upland Luzon, it is hydroelectric dams. For the Montagnards of Vietnam, it is robusta coffee farms. For the forest Tiboli of Indonesia's remote Halmahera island, it is nickel mines. Everywhere it is the same. Meanwhile, as the long arms of the global marketplace reach deep into Southeast Asia, so do the tax collectors, engineers, and schoolteachers of the region's national governments, asserting their claims of sovereignty over far-flung and disparate citizens and their valuable resources. Armies also play a role, keeping restive minorities in check and disciplining, often by use of violence, the state's claim to power.

In this climate of tectonic change, millions of people are on the move, shifting from forests into timber and mining camps, from villages into towns, and from towns into cities and megacities. Great numbers are migrating across national borders to seek work in neighboring countries. Tens of thousands every year are being trafficked as sex workers, domestic servants, and fishing-fleet boatmen. Others are fleeing violence and harassment into refugee camps and to new homes abroad. Southeast Asia is static only on the map.

Complicating these large forces is a mind-boggling heterogeneity of languages, dialects, ethnicities, religions, and customs. In Southeast Asia, multiple complex societies exist side by side. These societies have been shaped by centuries of interaction not only with each other but also with India and China and, in recent centuries, with newcomers from the West—the Portuguese,

Spanish, Dutch, English, French, and Americans, whose colonies in the region prefigured today's nation-states. The region's complex roots and its contemporary character are belied by the simplicity of the map and of popular perceptions. We talk glibly of Burmese, Filipinos, Indonesians, and Thais as though they were essential human types. Likewise, we speak of Thailand, Cambodia, Vietnam, and Singapore as entities fixed in time. These are convenient constructions, it is true, but, as in all such constructions, they mask complex realities.

Snapshots from the neighborhood

Today, all of Southeast Asia's countries conform to the model of the nation-state. Yet as nation-states they are remarkably different. Some are democratic federations and republics, others are "people's democratic republics," still others are kingdoms. They are led by prime ministers, presidents, party secretaries, sultans, and kings. As national societies, writ large, they are Muslim, Buddhist, and Christian. Two are officially Marxist. But they contain within them adherents of almost every other religion on earth as well as legions of spirit and ancestor cults—since even in these most modern of times, the spirits must be attended to. Each country in its unique way is typically Southeast Asian.

Among the predominantly Buddhist countries of the mainland, Thailand stands out as the largest by territory and second largest by population (*c.* 69 million in 2017). It is significantly more prosperous than its neighbors. A sometime democracy and oftentimes a military-led state, it coalesces around the memory of its famous nineteenth-century kings and its still-revered royal family. Cunning political actors, Thai elites avoided overt colonialism (the only Southeast Asian kingdom to do so), dodged the ravages of World War II by collaborating with Japan, and maneuvered astutely through the dangerous years of the Cold War by aligning themselves with the United States. Thailand's gross domestic product (GDP) per capita is on the rise, its strong economy is drawing migrants from neighboring countries, and its middle class is blossoming. Its capital, Bangkok, shines as a leading Southeast Asian mega city with a vibrant arts scene, business sector, and an alluring cosmopolitan face, including its smiling generals.

Meanwhile, Thailand's neighbor to the west, Myanmar (Burma), a Buddhist society much like Thailand with a population almost as large, paints a different picture. By the numbers, it is one of Southeast Asia's poorest. (Thailand's GDP per capita is seven times higher.) Once a proud kingdom like Thailand, its nineteenth-century kings were defeated by British armies and then banished as Burma was subsumed within the British Empire. It was a heavily contested theater of war in World War II, when its emergent national leaders both collaborated with and resisted the Japanese. With independence in 1948 came a dysfunctional democracy, then decade upon decade of military rule under Ne Win and his development program that wedded Buddhism and socialism. By the 1980s, Burma was backward, isolated, and riven by armed rebellions. A democracy movement led by Aung San Suu Kyi and subsequent political and economic reforms in recent years have weakened the grip of the army, ended the country's isolation, and brought elected governments to power, alongside a flood of new investments. Yet the house of Myanmar remains bitterly divided. As the world is rushing in, hundreds of thousands of Myanmar's beleaguered minority subjects are taking desperate measures to rush out.

Cambodia, to the east of Thailand, is the site of one of Southeast Asia's monstrous modern atrocities. The dark clouds of the Khmer Rouge and their "Killing Fields" (1975–1978) still hang over the nation today. Heirs of the once-monumental kingdom of Angkor (800s–1400s), Cambodia's kings of the nineteenth century attempted to steer their much-diminished kingdom to safety under French protection. Cambodia thus entered the twentieth century and the travails of World War II as part of French

Indochina with its residual monarchy neutered but intact. Hence it was a king, Norodom Sihanouk, who, repackaged as a president, took over when France departed in 1953 and who attempted to steer his small Buddhist kingdom to safety through the treacherous shoals of the Cold War, including the hot war in neighboring Vietnam. His failure and intensive U.S. bombing in Cambodia led directly to the triumph of the Khmer Rouge and the murder and manslaughter of more than two million people and, after 1979, to a long recuperation involving occupation by both Vietnam and the United Nations. Cambodia survives today as a small Buddhist kingdom of 16 million people with a constitutional monarch—Sihanouk's son—and a quasi-elected strongman prime minister who is also a former Khmer Rouge commander.

In Thailand, Burma, and Cambodia today, national leaders invoke the language of democracy and representative government even though in practice this remains largely an aspiration. Thailand is ruled, off and on, by an army junta; in Myanmar and Cambodia elections are held, but one might say that democracy as it is practiced remains highly compromised by authoritarian power structures. Southeast Asia's two other mainland states are unapologetically one-party states.

Modern Laos, a traditionally Buddhist society much like its neighbors, was formed from an amalgamation of princely domains into another French protectorate in the 1890s. The colony's affiliation with French Indochina drew it into Vietnam's long war for independence, which ended after years of confusion and turmoil in 1975 with a government led by the Communist Party in both countries. One of the quieter corners of Southeast Asia, the Lao People's Democratic Republic remains a highly agrarian and still largely Buddhist society where the largest city, Vientiane, hosts fewer than 1 million people. The former royal capital at Luang Prabang, upriver from Vientiane and much smaller, is renowned for its grace. The lowland Lao majority populates the country's narrow river valleys, yet a full 90 percent of the country's territory rises above 600 feet and is populated by non-Lao, swidden-farming hill peoples. Today, the long arm of globalization is reaching deep into Laos from every side, including from China, the country with which it shares a porous 263-mile-long border.

Vietnam's independence movement led by the Communists under Ho Chi Minh and its eventual triumph over both France and the United States is a legendary epic in modern Southeast Asian history. This is how the once domineering Confucian kingdom of Vietnam, humiliated and colonized by France in the nineteenth century, abandoned its feudal trappings to rise as Southeast Asia's strongest and, today with more than 95 million people, largest Communist state. Vietnam's victorious revolutionary struggle gave its Communist Party great authority, and the party rules up until now, despite having long since abandoned many tenets of communist ideology. In today's fast-changing Vietnam, the market is in full play and old enemies are becoming new allies.

In island Southeast Asia, Indonesia dominates. With a population of more than 263 million people, it is not only the largest country in Southeast Asia but the fourth-largest country in the world. This far-flung archipelago once hosted literally hundreds of kingdoms before being patched together into a massive tropical colony by the Dutch—a project that took three hundred years. In the early twentieth century young nationalists reimagined the Dutch East Indies as Indonesia. Through the violent interruption of World War II and after four years of revolution, in 1949 it came to be. Islam is the dominant religious culture here. And among the country's hundreds of ethnicities, the Javanese rule the roost.

Like Cambodia, Indonesia also became the site of mass killings during the region's wrenching left-right power struggles of the Cold War era. In Cambodia, Communists were the perpetrators. In Indonesia, in 1965, Communists were the victims, with some 500,000 party members and affiliates dead in army-led executions and massacres that lasted months. The military regime that followed continued for more than thirty years but it has been followed by a substantial new experiment in democracy. This includes, these days, suspenseful, hotly contested multiparty elections.

Two of Indonesia's near neighbors in the same great archipelago, Malaysia and Singapore, also owe their modern configurations to European empire-building. These territories—including the Malay Peninsula and adjacent islands as well as a large swath of northern Borneo—were cobbled together piecemeal by generations of builders of the British Empire. The territories included several Malay sultanates or mini-kingdoms, two privately held colonial domains in Borneo under British protection (Sarawak and Sabah), and two offshore island trade emporiums populated largely by Chinese migrants and other newcomers that were created by the British (Singapore and Penang). As Britain retreated from empire following World War II, it fashioned this odd collection of colonial remnants into a nation-state called Malaysia. In 1965, Singapore, the larger, richer, and most conspicuously Chinese of the trade hubs, subsequently withdrew to strike out on its own. The others have become today's Federation of Malaysia, another of Southeast Asia's authoritarian democracies in which a single political party dominates in collaboration with multisectarian coalition partners. A constitutional monarch is the symbolic face of the nation: Malaysia's king is a Malay sultan. One of Southeast Asia's smaller states, at 31 million, Malaysia is also one of its more prosperous ones, with a GDP per capita twice that of Thailand.

But Singapore is far richer. Indeed, Singapore's GDP per capita tops that of the United States. An anomaly in Southeast Asia as a predominantly ethnic Chinese city-state, Singapore is also one of the region's smallest countries, with six million people. Politically, it is a parliamentary democracy in which a single party wholly dominates. The People's Action Party (PAP) has no coalition partners. This has been true since Singapore's founding days under Lee Kuan Yew, the island nation's extraordinary prime minister, founder of the PAP, architect of the country's remarkable rise, and author of its unique way of doing things in which Confucianism, capitalism, socialism, and state-sponsored social engineering all play a part.

The final major nation of island Southeast Asia is anomalous in another way. Spain aggregated the islands of Southeast Asia's other large archipelago more than four hundred years ago and called the new entity *Las Philipinas* (the Philippines), after King Philip II. Under Spanish sway, the archipelago's lowland people adapted Christianity and evolved as a Southeast Asian society with considerable Spanish influence until being seized by the United States at the turn of the twentieth century. The Philippines today, with more than 103 million people, reflects this dual heritage. It is flamboyantly democratic and election-loving and at the same time strikingly oligarchic, with a governing class whose members compete aggressively with each other for public office and seldom yield power to the masses below. In the Philippines, elite-led democracy has proved stronger than dictatorship, an option famously tested by Ferdinand Marcos beginning in 1972 and rejected in a popular nonviolent mass movement led by Corazon Aquino in 1986. Subsequent elected presidents have included a retired general, a movie star, and the daughter of one former president and the son of another (Aquino's son, Benigno Aquino III) as well as the strong-arm populist Rodrigo Duterte, yet another scion of the governing class.

Two countries remain. The sultanate of Brunei, which rests in a tiny molar-shaped pocket of territory surrounded by Malaysian Borneo, is all that remains of a kingdom that once was much larger. But that which remains rests on one of the richest oil and gas deposits in Asia, making tiny Brunei, population 500,000, a source of stupendous wealth both for its sultan and the royal family and for Brunei Shell Petroleum. Once a British protectorate like its immediate neighbors, the sultanate declined Britain's offer to join Malaysia and carries on today as Southeast Asia's only remaining absolute monarchy.

East Timor, or Timor-Leste, is not so lucky. Occupying the eastern half of the island of Timor in the eastern Indonesian archipelago and with a per capital income of less than U.S. $4,000, it has few resources and little wealth. Evolving for centuries as a remote outpost of Portugal's increasingly impoverished empire, East Timor was jolted into the contemporary world in 1975 when Portugal moved out and Indonesia moved in, claiming the territory as a province. Its current generation of leadership emerged under the turmoil and brutality of the unwelcome Indonesian occupation and the small country's eventual liberation in 1999 and full sovereignty in 2002.

Even this poor, remote, and small Southeast Asian country illustrates the region's underlying pluralism and complex entanglements with the wider world. The 1.2 million people of East Timor comprise ten and more distinct Malayo-Polynesian and Papuan ethnic groups spread across a hilly, hardscrabble terrain. Sixteen indigenous languages are spoken in addition to the vernacular lingua franca, Tetum. During the recent twenty-nine-year Indonesian occupation, many people also learned to speak Indonesian. Today, they are learning English. Even so, the country's small elite chose Portuguese as the official national language. The Roman Catholic Church claims 90 percent of the population, yet everywhere local spirits vie with the saints for people's devotion. Aside from some coffee, cinnamon, and cocoa, East Timor's modern economy produces little for the world's hungry markets, and its hopes for prosperity lie offshore in oil and gas deposits that are also claimed by Australia. With global markets in mind, the country's leaders have adopted as its national currency the U.S. dollar.

Southeast Asia and the world

These quick portraits of today's Southeast Asian countries reveal the degree to which they have been shaped by engagements with the wider world. In modern times, the expansive powers of the West have played the dominant role. But geography is destiny. Over the long haul nearby states and civilizations in Asia have played a greater role. The archipelagos, waterways, and riverine lowlands of Southeast Asia lie adjacent to, and exposed to, two of the world's great radiating civilizations. Traffic from India and China began early in history and has remained constant through the centuries. The Straits of Melaka have been a heavily traveled maritime passageway for two thousand years. Southeast Asians established harbor-town entrepôts to capture this trade. Through them the luxury goods of India and China penetrated the region's inland kingdoms, along with new gods and goddesses, art forms, languages, and words.

Southeast Asians were especially attracted to India's civilizations and borrowed heavily over many centuries, shaping innumerable aspects of Southeast Asia today. During the same centuries, China's merchants penetrated from the north bearing porcelains, silks, useful tools, and everyday objects to Southeast Asian harbor towns large and small. In these entrepôts, the goods of India and China changed hands alongside the spices, aromatic oils and woods, birds' nests, sea slugs, and pearls that Southeast Asians themselves brought to the market. No Indian kingdom ruled territories in Southeast Asia, but several Chinese dynasties occupied the Vietnamese homeland of Dai Viet for a thousand years before the Vietnamese broke away in 939 CE, placing an indelible Chinese stamp on the independent kingdom that emerged. China also pressed into the small kingdoms along Southeast Asia's northernmost tier and accepted tribute from others farther south on the mainland and in the islands, including the tiny gold-rich kingdom of Butuan in the south Philippine Archipelago, which sent five missions to China in the early 1000s.

The wave of Western imperialism in the modern era hemmed in the power of China for more than one hundred years and brought India wholly within the British Empire. Even so, during these same years migration from China to Southeast Asia greatly expanded, profoundly altering the region's demography and economy. Today, a resurgent China is reprising its historical role in Southeast Asian commerce and also in asserting its regional preeminence. It is a primary trading partner of virtually every Southeast Asian country and the source of billions in investment annually. It looms large. More than India, it also figures centrally in Southeast Asia's security calculations.

Aside from Thailand, none of today's Southeast Asian nations existed as independent states seventy years ago. In 1945, each one was reeling in the wake of the dramatic rise and fall of imperial Japan, whose empire during World War II embraced all of Southeast Asia. After the war, some of Southeast Asia's newly independent nations formed security alliances with their former colonizers. This was true of the Philippines, which in 1954 joined the United States–led Cold War pact called the Southeast Asia Treaty Organization (SEATO), alongside Thailand, which also placed itself within the anticommunist camp. Malaysia and Singapore did the same in alliance with Britain through the Five Power Defence Arrangements (FPDA).

In Vietnam, after being rebuffed by the United States, Ho Chi Minh aligned his eventually successful revolutionary movement and the post-1954 Democratic Republic of (North) Vietnam with the Soviet Union and China, even as the post-1954 state of South Vietnam was supported and defended by the United States and its regional allies. Meanwhile, others took a neutral path and declared themselves nonaligned. Alongside Burma, these countries included Cambodia and Indonesia, whose famously mercurial leaders Sihanouk and Sukarno, respectively played to both sides in the great global rift.

The 1965 massacres of Communists in Indonesia and the onset of military rule under Suharto, following Sukarno's fall, led to a significant shift. Suharto quickly brought his country into the U.S.-led anti-communist orbit. This set the stage for the region's first successful regional organization. In 1967, Indonesia, together with Thailand, Malaysia, Singapore, and the Philippines, formed the Association of Southeast Asian Nations (ASEAN). The association was emphatically not a security alliance; rather, it was formed as a platform for mutual cooperation. Through its early meetings and nascent committee structure, the five disparate countries began working out many of the practical aspects of living in one neighborhood, such as aligning their postal services, air traffic control, and telecommunications.

ASEAN's founding members signed the Treaty of Amity and Cooperation in 1976 that struck at the heart of their security fears: they pledged to respect each other's sovereignty and to renounce the use of force in their relations with each other. This became the basis for the "ASEAN Way," an approach to resolving differences that avoided confrontation and favored patience over haste. What happens inside your borders is your business, not your neighbor's business. What cannot be agreed upon will be postponed. Although following the ASEAN Way meant that problem-solving could be glacial, it also meant that on the existential matter of state sovereignty member states could feel safe with one another. This proved to be a great boon.

At first and for many years, ASEAN represented Southeast Asia's anticommunist club; the sultanate of Brunei joined in 1984 upon its independence from Britain. But as the fate of Vietnam was resolved after 1975 and the fires of the Cold War eventually abated, the usefulness of the organization and the value of its philosophy became apparent to other members of the neighborhood. The communist states and other outliers all applied to join. Vietnam was first in 1995 followed by Laos and Myanmar in 1997 and Cambodia in 1999. East Timor awaits membership.

In the intervening years, ASEAN has served as the scaffolding for an elaborate structure of diplomatic relations both among the member states and between the collective members and the rest of the world. ASEAN coordinates officially with China, Japan, and South Korea in ASEAN+3, and its dialogue partners in the annual ASEAN Regional Forum include the major powers of Europe, Asia, and the Americas. ASEAN enjoys observer status at the United Nations General Assembly, and in 2001 it became officially a nuclear-weapons-free zone. Although ASEAN's honor-thy-neighbor policy has thwarted some much-needed reforms, its tolerant philosophy has allowed the association to endure and remain relevant. Today it is the format through which the region is exploring more advanced levels of cooperation in areas such as free trade, labor exchanges, and a monetary union.

ASEAN is only one mechanism through which Southeast Asian countries seek security today. With an eye to China and to new security threats represented by terrorism, unruly population flows, and environmental alarms, many of the nations maintain close ties with the West and also cultivate good relations with China, Japan, and South Korea, which are important trading partners, aid givers, and potential diplomatic allies. Militarily, no Southeast Asian country is in a position to secure itself independently. Only Vietnam has raised a large standing army in recent history, and despite rising military budgets and larger fleets of (mostly aging, secondhand) warplanes and warships, none of them today possesses the wherewithal to stand alone. Instead, each one engages in a variety of balancing tactics designed both to engage with the large powers of the world, on the one hand, and to keep them at a distance, on the other.

In this process today, China is all important. All of Southeast Asia's countries welcome Chinese investments to a degree. Chinese goods pour across the porous borders of the mainland states and fill the provincial markets and city stores and malls. It is hardly different in the islands. Chinese private and state-connected companies are aggressively expanding in Southeast Asia in the mining, agribusiness, and tourism sectors as well as in transportation and hydroelectricity. (In Laos, where China accounts for 40 percent of foreign investment, Chinese companies are building casinos, five-star hotels, banana and rubber plantations, and dozens of hydroelectric dams.) Meanwhile, China is expanding its strategic presence into Southeast Asia in the South China Sea. Diplomacy can contain these mounting pressures to a degree, but momentum on the Chinese side and weak leverage on the Southeast Asian side make this penetration more or less unstoppable. China cannot be contained. It must be engaged.

These days, Southeast Asian officials meet with Chinese officials at every level, both bilaterally and through ASEAN's consultative structures. More significantly, Thailand, Indonesia, Singapore, Myanmar, Cambodia, Malaysia, and the Philippines have established military-to-military links with China to facilitate aid and loans, joint training exercises, and joint production of military equipment, as well as a forum for discussing security issues. China has claimed ASEAN as a strategic partner. In 2003 it signed ASEAN's foundational Treaty of Amity and Cooperation, pledging to eschew armed conflict and to respect the sovereignty and internal integrity of its neighbors.

At the same time, most of the ASEAN countries also have security ties with the United States and welcome the presence of the American Seventh Fleet, which patrols the all-important Melaka Straits and posts some twenty thousand military personnel in the region at any given time. Singapore serves as the logistics center of the American fleet and provides both its naval base and its airfields. Thailand, Indonesia, and Malaysia have signed military access agreements, and both Thailand and the Philippines have been granted special access to U.S. intelligence as major non-NATO allies. Under a visiting forces agreement signed in 1999, the Philippines has invited thousands of U.S. soldiers to assist in its war against Muslim separatists and to engage in war games. Indonesia is happy to buy advanced weapons from the United States under special agreement and sends its officers for training in the United States. Even Vietnam is slowly opening its ports to the American navy and receives a modest U.S. military aid package. (Vietnam continues to acquire most of its arms from Russia, however—another balancing strategy.) Meanwhile, Britain and other members of the Five Power Defence Arrangements continue to support Malaysia.

Writ large, these complex arrangements balancing China and the United States (and other powers such as Great Britain, Japan, and Russia) are not designed with specific quid pro quos in mind, although much fine print is involved. Their real purpose is to create a web of interlocking and overlapping alliances and relationships that mitigates against predatory behavior and the resort to force. This is a familiar Southeast Asian approach to things. When trouble looms, rally your friends. Indonesian president Joko Widodo was not being glib when he described his country's foreign policy as "a thousand friends and no enemies."

Elites and national economies

The governing classes in Southeast Asia today have their roots in the deep past and also in more recent history. Lineage matters in Southeast Asia. In Thailand, Malaysia, and Cambodia constitutional monarchies reveal the contemporary appeal of aristocracy. Princes and princesses and hierarchies of titled people continue to exist. In Thailand, virtually all of the country's elected and nonelected leaders (conspicuously its power-seizing generals) pledge their loyalty to the king. In Malaysia, a parliamentary democracy, all but one of the country's prime ministers since independence has hailed from a royal lineage. In places where these feudal trappings have been officially abandoned, such as Indonesia, politicians and even military dictators routinely claim aristocratic roots. Sukarno did so, as did Suharto, through his wife. The Philippines lacks such an aristocracy but most of its leading politicians descend from wealthy provincial clans whose preeminence dates from Spanish times. Indeed, virtually everywhere in the region, many of today's elites are descendants of families that have enjoyed privileged status for generations, if not for centuries.

The colonial states that dominated Southeast Asia until World War II did not supplant indigenous elites; they subordinated them. Everywhere members of upper-class families continued to serve as officials in the colonial states. More importantly, colonial regimes generally limited education in Western languages and advanced subjects to members of high-status families. (This is how Sukarno became a Dutch-speaking engineer and how Tunku Abdul Rahman became an English-speaking lawyer.) This status enabled them to come forward as modern leaders in the twentieth century—to lead reformist and nationalist movements and, at independence, to become the governing classes of the region's new nations. (Sukarno as Indonesia's founding president, Tunku Abdul Rahman as the founding prime minister of Malaysia.) Independence and the advent of military rule opened new paths to political leadership; as armies became institutionalized and matured, officer corps merged into the governing classes in Burma, Thailand, and Indonesia. In Vietnam and also in Laos, it was the Communist Party that offered new avenues to power, as senior cadres and their families formed the country's new elite.

These people of high status emerged as governing classes in societies with largely agrarian economies and only rudimentary processing and manufacturing sectors. For the most part, they themselves and their families were not people of business. They tended to draw their wealth and incomes from landed properties, rent-seeking, and the perquisites of officialdom. For the most part, business and industry and the realm of money were the domains of Southeast Asians of Chinese descent. The roots of this phenomenon also lay in the colonial period when a combination of new opportunities in the Western colonies and catastrophes in China led hundreds of thousands of migrants to the region. Colonial laws and policies steered them away from rural landowning and into towns and cities, where they flourished as laborers, artisans, shopkeepers, and capitalists large and small. This occurred everywhere in Southeast Asia but was complemented in British domains by the arrival of Indians, who played similar roles but on a smaller scale. Chinese migrants became modern Southeast Asia's essential urbanites—Kuala Lumpur was founded by the mining camp boss Yap Ah Loy—and formed a distinctive commercial class.

The majority of these migrants were men, and their marriages to local women created mixed Chinese-Southeast Asian families everywhere. In the Philippines and Thailand, this mestizo class blended with high-status indigenous families and became an integral part of the nascent national elite. Corazon Cojuangco Aquino, former president of the Philippines, is exemplary of this important trend: her great-grandfather was a certain Co Yu Hwan, who migrated to the Spanish Philippines from China in the nineteenth century. Her family and many others like it are quintessentially Filipino by culture. Elsewhere, the evolving Chinese and Chinese-mestizo communities remained distinctively apart. This is true in today's Malaysia, Indonesia, and Singapore. New migrations in the twentieth century and the arrival of ever larger numbers of Chinese women also created distinctively Chinese communities even in societies with a high level of assimilation, so that we may speak of Chinese Filipinos, Sino-Thai, and Sino-Vietnamese.

The pride of place of the Chinese in the region's economy and the community's conspicuous well-being compared with the region's indigenous majorities have long been sore points. A common feature of policies following World War II in many Southeast Asian countries has been an attempt to use the powers of government to place more of the nation's wealth and potential wealth in the hands of its indigenous elites—and to enrich its indigenous populations as well. To a degree, they have succeeded.

Southeast Asians have long profited by participating in trade, introducing their own valuable products into the vital stream of commerce that connected India to China and to the wider world. (Cloves, which once grew only on a cluster of remote Southeast Asian islands, were mentioned in Pliny's *Natural History* [first century CE] and have been identified in the archaeological remains of an ancient Mesopotamian pantry.) Under European rule in recent centuries, commodities from Southeast Asia, such as coffee, sugar, tea, tobacco, and rubber, reached global markets alongside timber, minerals, and petroleum. Up until independence, the immense profits of this economy accrued mainly to the European and American capitalists, and their employees and shareholders, and to the local Chinese merchants, shippers, contractors, agents, and suppliers who made it logistically possible. For the most part, indigenous Southeast Asians participated in this economy as laborers, clerical workers, and small-time cash croppers and traders.

Following independence, Southeast Asian governing classes strove to redirect many of these profits to Southeast Asians themselves and, at the same time, to diversify their national economies by advancing manufacturing and other sectors. In this project, government has itself played a key role everywhere. By intervening directly in key sectors (such as rice, petroleum, and energy), licensing lucrative subsectors (importing automobiles, machinery, food additives, medicines), granting monopoly concessions to, say, harvest timber on government land or to establish telecommunication grids, and controlling access to loans from government banks and serving as brokers between foreign aid givers and local aid recipients, Southeast Asian governments and their regime elites have enriched themselves. They have also nourished their supporters through vast patronage networks connecting politicians, army generals, and dictators at the top to tiers of bureaucrats, officials, supplicant businesspeople, and party members on down to the lowest tiers, which, in some places, actually include voters.

Patron-client pyramids like this vary from society to society and regime to regime and take on new shapes and functions as rural people become city people, but in Southeast Asia today they underpin social structures everywhere. Built upon *personal* obligations and connections—who do you know?—they privilege loyalty over the law. They are vulnerable to nepotism, bribery, and other corruptions, but they are also highly resilient and flexible and make it possible for societies to cohere even as economies flounder and governments change. In democratic systems, patron-client pyramids realign after elections as new members of the governing class achieve top positions. They undergo major realignments with major regime changes. This occurred when Ferdinand Marcos seized power in the Philippines, for example, and when Suharto's dictatorship collapsed in Indonesia.

These underlying social constructs help to explain why Southeast Asia, despite many disruptions, is a relatively stable global region in which governing elites of various kinds seek prosperity and security by both co-opting and resisting the entreaties of greater powers—balancing this one against that one—and opportunistically manipulating access to the national economies.

Although in the early years of independence several Southeast Asian governments attempted to protect nascent home industries behind tariff walls in a strategy called import substitution, most of them eventually concluded that opening their economies to foreign investors paid higher dividends, as did prioritizing their historical strengths exporting commodities, minerals, and petroleum. Today commodities from Southeast Asia are pouring into China as well as into the rising economies of South Korea and Japan and the industrial West. This development is enriching many people in Southeast Asia, and it also accounts for the transformation of the region's environment.

Meanwhile, in most countries of the region, governments have also promoted industrialization and the growth of high-tech manufacturing that complements the resource sector and protects national economies against the vagaries of shifting global commodity prices. In Thailand, the Philippines, Malaysia, and Indonesia—Southeast Asia's newly industrialized countries (NICs)—these sectors are advanced. In Singapore they are so advanced, alongside cutting-edge banking and financial services, that the country is one of the richest in the world as measured by GDP per capita and other measures. (The Sultanate of Brunei is rich for another reason.) A huge gap separates Singapore from Malaysia, the second most prosperous country in the region, and a large gap again separates Malaysia from the other NICs. Burma, Cambodia, Laos, and East Timor remain poor by any standard, with a large majority of their populations still bound to the land and only nascent modern sectors. Even so, in each one, resource extraction in the form of logging, hydroelectricity, raw materials, and, in Burma's case, petroleum, is generating wealth for rulers and their clients as new investments from China are drawing even these slow-growing states into the needy matrix of globalization.

The rich complexities of modern Southeast Asia—its radical heterogeneity; its hills and plains; its great cities and agricultural hinterlands; its dynamic engagement with the outside world; its presidents, prime ministers, domineering military men, and kings; and its asymmetrical prosperity—all have roots deep in history. Southeast Asia is unquestionably of the moment. It is modern, but it is modern in distinctively Southeast Asian ways.

Chapter 2
Kingdoms

Rice is the foundation of Southeast Asian life. The discovery of rice cultivation appears to have occurred in southern China. People living in Southeast Asia were its early adapters. By the second or third millennium BCE, they were growing rice, domesticating pigs, chickens, and cattle, and forming the region's earliest settled communities in several mainland areas congruent with present-day northern Vietnam, Thailand, and Malaya. By the 5th century BCE, they had become iron and bronze workers. Their large and elaborate funnel-shaped bronze drums decorated with frogs, birds, and warriors in long boats—often called Dong Son drums from a key archaeological site in northern Vietnam—became one of the region's first items of luxury trade and dispersed throughout much of Southeast Asia.

In these early centuries, people occupied particularly favorable niches of the region's habitat, taking advantage of abundant fish, fruits, and animal life as they formed settled rice-growing (and in places millet-, sago-, taro-, and yam-growing) communities. These people, alongside later arrivals, were the ancestors of today's Southeast Asians, whose small communities barely altered the landscape as they formed amid Southeast Asia's vast tropical forests.

We know little about the organization of these early societies or about how these early farmers and fisherfolk at some point first

2. Wet-rice farmers work in the paddy fields of Vietnam. For centuries past and until today, paddy fields have dominated the cultivated landscape of lowland Southeast Asia and supported its large sedentary populations.

morphed into nascent polities or mini-states under the leadership of local strongmen and their kin and allies. In these times when land was plentiful and people were few, the key to amassing power lay in controlling people, not in amassing territory. By *c.* 250–540 CE, a large early state had emerged in a coastal area adjacent to the lower Mekong River: Funan, Southeast Asia's first "recorded" kingdom, that is, recorded by Chinese observers, who may have been exaggerating. For practical purposes, Funan marks the beginning of Southeast Asia's political history.

From Funan and for many centuries afterward, evidence is strong that the vast majority of Southeast Asian polities were small and local, consisting of local lords and strongmen, petty kings, perhaps, ruling over pockets of population amid the domineering forest. Many of these early polities lay nested along the fertile plains of the Mekong, Chao Phraya, Irrawaddy, and Red Rivers, and along similar but shorter rivers that formed fertile plains in Java, Luzon, and other island sites. Other favored sites were river mouths and coastlines where abundant fish and opportunities to trade led to the establishment of early harbor towns augmented by nearby villages of farmers. Here and there, fertile upland valleys also hosted small states based on wet-rice farming and the presence of gold or gem mines and other resources. This occurred, for example, in West Sumatra and in the Shan and Thai highlands.

These early pockets of settled people may have been no larger than a few hundred or a few thousand people, although some grew larger; the permanence and fecundity of wet-rice farming made this possible. At any given time in these early centuries there may have been hundreds of such mini-states spread across the mainland and islands, each with a king or raja or, later, when Islam took hold in the islands, a sultan of its own. This pattern of extreme disaggregation reflected the radical heterogeneity of the people themselves, with their hundreds of languages and dialects and emerging ethnicities. Such small polities were the norm.

But occasionally, one such king or strong man succeeded in establishing domination over a larger area by conquering or otherwise subordinating his neighbors, thus making a larger kingdom from several smaller ones, that is, by subordinating more people to himself. And thus, amid a vast realm of small states, some larger ones rose that came to dominate entire river valleys and their plains, or a network of affiliated harbor towns or coastal communities. And a few of these grew to become truly large states or empires. For the most part, it is only these that we know much about.

Funan appears to have been the first of these and dominated the lower Mekong River basin in the first centuries of the Common Era. By the 700s and 800s CE, kings of the Sailendra dynasty had created a great densely populated kingdom in central Java and built immense and beautiful monuments in stone. (Borobudur and Prambanan are their legacy.) Between the 700s and 1200s, powerful rulers based at Palembang in southern Sumatra ruled a vast sea-based thalassocracy known as Srivijaya that controlled the Straits of Melaka by dominating the surrounding coastal and harbor-town polities. And by 900 or so, the Khmer kings of Angkor had achieved domination over the rice plains of the Tonle Sap and lower Mekong basin in the great kingdom of classical Cambodia that prevailed in varying degrees of strength from the late 800s to the 1400s; their architectural legacy is the monumental temple complex of Angkor. By the time of Angkor, Vietnam (Dai Viet), which controlled the Red River delta of northern Vietnam, had already evolved as a frontier territory of China for nearly a thousand years. It broke free to stand on its own in 939.

In subsequent centuries, other large states emerged in ecologically predictable sites—along the Irrawaddy River basin and delta (kingdoms of Mons, Burmans, and Pyus); along the Chao Phraya River (the Thai); along the central Vietnam coast (Chams); and again in Java (the great Javanese kingdom of Majapahit [1300–1500]) and the Melaka Straits (Malay Melaka). Although the physical and literary remains of these big kingdoms dominate the historical record, we should understand them as only part of a wider pattern in which a few big states like these nested amid hundreds of smaller ones—with the autonomy of the smaller, peripheral ones either losing or gaining in relation to the constant waxing and waning of the larger ones, and with hill peoples always on the periphery.

A world of mandalas

The concept of the mandala helps us to explain this dynamic political world. Indians of the classical age adopted this image to visualize the world and the cosmos; Kautilya used it in his famous Arthashastra (*c.* 300 BCE) to discuss diplomacy and war. Southeast Asians borrowed the concept and the Sanskrit term from them. Think of a small circle that is encircled by increasingly larger and potentially infinite concentric circles. The circles represent a kingdom. Power rests in the center, the site of the capital and the locale of the king and his core officials and also of the kingdom's core population of farmers, urbanites, and slaves over which the ruler exercises power directly and whose labor and food production—through compulsion, taxation, and religious donations—forms the economic basis of the state. Here also, in the center, dwell the holy men and scholars of the king's religious cult and the artisans, musicians, and scribes who embellish the capital with monuments, music, and (a veneer of) literacy.

In what we shall call a mandala kingdom, the king's power radiated out from the capital and, as it passed by degree through each successive concentric circle, attenuated and eventually died out altogether or overlapped with the outer circles of another mandala—all without crossing any clear border. In the outer circles of his mandala, a king may not have controlled or drawn resources from people directly but, rather, indirectly through local lords and strong men. These vassals professed loyalty and rendered tribute, taxes, soldiers, and slaves to the center as long as the ruler was strong enough to coerce them. But they may have stinted on their obligations or broken free altogether when the king was weak and ruled as independent mini-kings over their own domains of followers and resources. Or, perhaps, they may have been sucked into the orbit of a competing mandala whose gravity pulled from another direction. Keep in mind that in Southeast Asia, adjacent mandalas may well have involved different ethnicities; the underlying tensions of mandala politics was more than a raw power struggle.

One can think of premodern Southeast Asia as a world of mandala kingdoms, large and small, with the larger mandalas expanding and contracting by absorbing their smaller neighbors into their orbits and contracting when outlying domains subsequently wrested free, and with the large mandalas competing with other

Southeast Asia

3. Premodern Southeast Asia through c. 1800.

PREMODERN SOUTHEAST ASIA

CHINA

Pacific
Ocean

South
China
Sea

Luzon

SIEM RIEP AND
BATTAMBANG

CHAMPA

Manila

Butuan/Agusan

Mindanao

Brunei

Ternate and
Tidore

Halmahera

New
Guinea

Borneo

Sulawesi

Ambon

Banda
Islands

Demak
Java Surakarta
yakarta

Bali

large mandalas for domination of their large domains and populations. This occurred, for example, in great wars between the Burmans and the Thais in the 18th century.

We think of Southeast Asia's mandala chiefs as "men of prowess." Their skills included not only prowess in war but also prowess in mobilizing followers to develop and sustain agricultural resources (in complex wet-rice regimes, for example), to engage in trade, and to execute essential religious rites. They were what we might today call entrepreneurs, and also politicians in the sense that their prowess involved superior rhetorical skills and diplomatic acumen. In the turbulent world of competing mandalas, high royal birth placed one in competition for power but did not guarantee it. Kings had many sons, not to mention brothers and legions of royal cousins. Queens and their progeny formed factions at court and intrigued for position; occasionally, they ruled. Succession disputes were routine and often violent. It was men of prowess (and on occasion women) who prevailed.

The power of a Southeast Asian mandala's king was measured in part by the size and splendor of his capital with its monuments and royal trappings and public pageantry designed to glorify the king and his cult. All this was embellished with tiers of officials and priests and scribes, soldiers, artisans, and other urbanites and the sea of the capital's immediate supporting population of farmers and slaves. Smaller kings ruling smaller mandalas attempted to mimic this display of power with similar elements of grandeur on a lesser scale. Underlying such displays of power were the relationships of deference and loyalty that linked the lords of outlying circles of the mandala, or the lords of smaller mandalas that were satellites of a greater one, to the center.

Coercion was a factor. Small states were conquered and seized by neighboring larger ones. But diplomacy also played a part. A mandala lord might simply acknowledge his deference to the center by sending gifts and tribute—Malay sultans sent gold flowers (*bunga mas*) to the Siamese king. He might contribute men to the king's armies. Or he might send one of his daughters or sisters to become one of the king's royal wives, thus cementing a power relationship with a family one. Such relationships, we assume, varied case by case, each one in a more or less constant process of negotiation as the screws tightened when the dominant ruler was strong and loosened when he was weak.

In smaller mandala kingdoms, Southeast Asian rulers presided over populations of farmers, slaves, and urban folk in a single niche habitat along a river, at a river mouth or favorable coastal site, or a

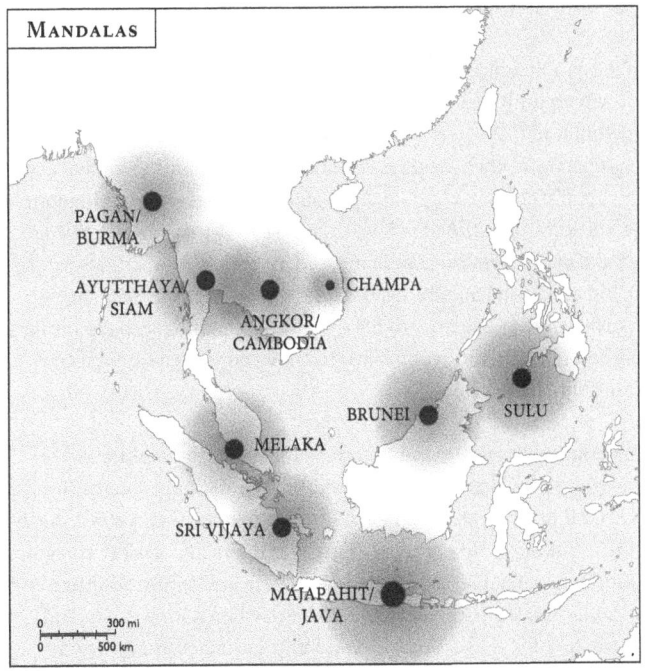

4. In Southeast Asia's mandala kingdoms—conceptualized abstractly in this map—the king's power radiated out from the capital, diminished with distance, and eventually died out without crossing any clear border.

fertile upland valley (as in the Yunnan–Southeast Asia cusp of northern Burma, Laos, and Vietnam). Here management of the realm could be more or less direct and executed by loyal kin and officials who answered directly to the king. But as the mandala expanded, taking in the territories of neighboring leaders and rival ethnicities, controlling the realm involved indirect arrangements in which local lords and their families and other elites (and their ways of doing things) were incorporated into the power structure of the large mandala, where they might remain only briefly or for several generations. Aside from establishing family ties between rulers and vassals through marriage, patron-client calculations applied in which the advantages of loyalty to the center were weighed against the costs of lost resources and the sting of deference.

One can imagine the immense complexity of large mandala states in which multiple satellite societies were linked to the center through multifarious ties of—almost always—reluctant vassalage. Larger states that dominated their regions for long periods gradually developed relatively sophisticated systems of kingdom-wide administration. Such was the case in Burma during the age of Pagan, in Ayutthaya in Siam, and, of course, in Vietnam, where China provided an advanced model. But always beneath the surface lurked the underlying dynamics of mandala contestation. When the larger kingdoms fragmented, they fragmented into familiar smaller ones.

The mandala world was therefore inherently unstable, as neighboring kingdoms small and large invariably sought to expand at the expense of each other. Violence was a constant in the form of raiding and slaving on land and sea. Power struggles among a ruler's large coterie of brothers and sons and other pretenders led to crises and civil wars when a king died. And occasionally, powerful mandala kings launched major wars against their neighbors that involved great armies of foot soldiers and war elephants (such as those rendered in stone on the walls of Angkor Wat).

In all of these encounters, the object was the same: to bring larger numbers of people into the domain of the winner. Followers equaled power. War captives were literally taken to the victor's capital. Perhaps for this reason, mandala kings preferred war strategies that mitigated against slaughter—overpowering the enemy with shock and awe, for example, or determining the outcome by way of elephant-mounted dueling princes. Even so, we can be certain there was plenty of slaughter and other destruction and insecurity when great armies took to the field and as the routine power struggles and predatory raiding of the mandala world swept over the region's settled communities. Southeast Asians adapted to these threats by moving, literally by abandoning a dangerous site for a safe one farther away. Others fled the dangers and oppressions of the mandala-dominated lowlands for safety in the region's inaccessible hills and mountains.

As a way of thinking about the myriad kingdoms and mini-kingdoms of Southeast Asia's long early history, the mandala concept applies both to the mainland and to the islands, where a ruler's mandala domain might extend no farther than a single island or two, or the lower reaches of a river (on, say, Borneo or Malaya or Sumatra) and a raja's capital at the mouth of the river. Or it might encompass several islands or harbor-town capitals and their lowland interiors, as in the great Melaka Straits mandala thalassocracy of Srivijaya or those of the sultans of Brunei or Sulu that aggregated mini-states linked by bodies of water instead of land. The mandala concept also applies to Vietnam (Dai Viet) in the early centuries, although as rulers who followed China's model, Vietnam's kings did embrace the existence of explicit borders (especially its border with China) in a way that other Southeast Asian rulers did not.

The lure of Indian civilization

These early Southeast Asian societies and states did not evolve in isolation; rather, they did so in communication with adjacent Asian civilizations in India and China. The idea of the mandala itself came from India and, for the most part, the emerging societies of the mandala world of Southeast Asia world sought to base their own rising civilizations on the older, deeper one of nearby India.

By the time of Funan, the awe-inspiring cosmos and complex spiritual culture of myriad gods and goddesses and profound philosophical ideas of the Hindu world were a thousand years old. Buddhism, an offshoot of the Hindu world, had also been evolving for hundreds of years, and between 268 and 232 BCE a great Buddhist king, Ashoka, had united virtually the entire continent and created the greatest Indian mandala yet in history. Traffic between Indian states and harbor towns and early Southeast Asian polities was already well established by the time of Funan, whose kings claimed descent from an Indian Brahmin and organized their farming communities around tanks or reservoirs, India-style. A great wave of Indianization had begun. In the following centuries, key elements of Indian religious life, arts, and language as well as law and statecraft and countless stories of heroes and villains, gods and men, and fantastical beings drifted into the region borne by merchants and holy men and travelers of all kinds, including legions of itinerant experts known as brahmins. They were embraced by Burmans and Javanese, Khmers and Chams, Thais and Malays, and countless other Southeast Asian peoples who aspired to be a part of the great civilization of India and the vast Hindu-Buddhist world.

Proof for this is to be found in a proliferation of archaeological evidence, from the great stone monuments of Borobudur in Java and Angkor Wat in Cambodia to the thousands of smaller monuments and statues, text-bearing stiles, and stone, bronze, silver, and gold figures that have been found scattered across the region as far as the remotest islands of the Philippine archipelago. But there is abundant historical and living evidence as well—religious and literary texts and law codes, genealogies, and court documents plus India-derived alphabets, words, and stories, not to mention place-names, personal names, and legions of decorative patterns, sacred symbols, and common rituals in play up until today.

In the Indianized states of Southeast Asia, kings became *devaraja,* or god-kings, and represented themselves as incarnations of Hindu deities such as Siva and Vishnu or as Buddhist monarchs in the manner of Ashoka, or as revered bodhisattvas such as Avalokitesvara (e.g., at the Bayon temple of Angkor). Their mandala kingdoms mirrored the India-conceived cosmos itself, with great temple "mountains" dominating the mandala center—depictions of Mount Meru, the mythical home of the gods around which the world revolves. The stupendous Buddhist stupa at Borobudur is an eighth-century legacy of the Sailendra kingdom of Mataram, a multitiered monument that honored Buddha and also displayed the piety and power of its king. Its architectural plan in which tiers of concentric square and round terraces (adorned with exquisite Buddha images) rise like a pyramid to a single bell-shaped stupa at the top is a precise depiction of a mandala. Nearby, about thirty miles (fifty kilometers) away, is Prambanan, another monumental temple complex and mandala center of subsequent kings in which the main temple honors Siva alongside somewhat smaller ones honoring Vishnu and Brahma, the other two gods of the Hindu Trimurti, or trinity; here, too, are representations in stone of a wide pantheon of Hindu gods and mythical beings, including Ganesha, Nandi, and Rama.

These two temple complexes, one Buddhist and one Hindu, were built only one hundred years apart. This fact illustrates how Southeast Asians partook of Hinduism and Buddhism more or less simultaneously and why we commonly refer to this long period of Indianization as a Hindu-Buddhist era. The temple complex of Angkor in Cambodia contains both the Hindu temple honoring Siva and Vishnu known as Angkor Wat and, just a few miles away, the great Bayon temple complex in which Bodhisattva Avalokitesvara (and King Jayavarman VII) looks out in all directions from the king's mandala center. The great plain of

Buddhist temples and stupas at Pagan in present-day Myanmar is another monumental mandala center.

Drawing upon the great traditions of India, Southeast Asians had many options to choose from. We can imagine that persuasive Hindu brahmins and Buddhist monks led them to one cult or sect or another, with the result that a great profusion of practices occurred within the larger Hindu-Buddhist discourse, including tantric and occult practices (in Java, for example) and original fusions of India's great traditions with local ones in which ancestral and strictly local spirits were carefully honored and appeased.

Belief in such spirits—the anima or life in all things—forms the original, primal form of spirituality in Southeast Asia. Even as Southeast Asians adapted Hindu and Buddhist (and later Muslim and Christian) beliefs and practices, they never wholly abandoned the deep belief that, for example, rice is alive and that the songs of

5. Angkor Wat is part of a monumental temple complex marking the center of the great Khmer mandala of Southeast Asia's age of kingdoms.

birds, the sudden chills of a breeze, and the stirring of volcanoes bear messages. In the twelfth-century Thai kingdom of Sukhothai, King Ram Khamhaeng devoted his realm to Buddha, whose statues adorned the cardinal points of his mandala capital (we are told this in a famous inscription), but he did not neglect to honor the powerful local spirit of Phra Khaphung, "superior to all the spirits of the country." In Java, Brahma, Siva, and Vishnu and their retinues did not erase or replace local gods such as Roro Kidul, Javanese goddess of the Southern Seas. Wise rulers honored one and all.

As elements of Indian civilization penetrated Southeast Asia, they did so unevenly and serendipitously, creating hybridities of endless variation as attractive elements of the "new" from India fused with deeply rooted elements of the "old," i.e., hallowed local traditions. Southeast Asians borrowed heavily but not indiscriminately. And they never did so wholly. The Javanese and the Khmer and the Burman did not become Indians. They became new versions of themselves. This is a process that continues today.

In Indianized Southeast Asia, the great epics and story cycles of India became Southeast Asian stories: the Ramayana and the tale of Rama and his consort Sita and Hanuman the Monkey King (whose exploits were carved onto the bas-relief walls of both Prambanan and Angkor Wat) became the basis for countless retellings in drama and dance and stone. The Mahabharata brought the deep teachings of the Bhagavad Gita to Southeast Asia and became the basis for enduring popular arts, such as the Javanese shadow-puppet theater and its fantastical nightlong renderings of the epic war-of-cousins (Bharata Yudha) in which gods and men and demons play out their fated roles. The Jataka tales retell the lives of the Buddha in countless reincarnations leading up to enlightenment. They were carved in stone on the terraced walls of Borobudur in *c.* 800 and are recounted popularly throughout Burma, Thailand, Cambodia, and Laos today. Alongside the Ramayana and the Mahabharata, they became part of Southeast Asia's deep pool of stories and characters that formed the basis for its pervasive Hindu-Buddhist sense of the world.

These stories and their lessons and legions of characters provided the basis for every form of popular art and theater and also provided names of untold millions of Southeast Asians up to the present. King Ram Khamhaeng of Sukhothai (d. 1298), for example, was a fervent Buddhist king who bore a Hindu name: Rama. The same is true of all the kings of Thailand's reigning Chakri dynasty, each of whom, from the founder in 1782, has reigned as Rama. For centuries in Southeast Asia, people explained the highs and lows and many nuances of human nature and the vagaries of chance and history by retelling these stories and recounting the heroism, wisdom, and loyalty of the one and the villainy, cunning, and treachery of the other. Characters became archetypes: Ananda, the kind and selfless attendant of Buddha; Bima, the bold, action-seeking leader of the Mahabharata (and, in the twentieth century, Sukarno's own self-model as a young man.) And so on.

Along with stories and names came words. Very few Southeast Asians ever learned Sanskrit or Pali, the classical languages of Hinduism and Mahayana and Theravada Buddhism (Pali); this set of knowledge was limited to priestly classes. But Southeast Asians grafted thousands of Indian-origin words into their vernacular vocabularies. Indian words became Southeast Asian words in Malay, Javanese, Thai, Burmese, and other regional languages and even penetrated the Philippines. Early Spanish missionaries there discovered that lowland Filipinos used the word "Bhatala" for god, a direct cognate from Sanskrit (*bhattara*, lord). Today the common words for horse (*kuda*), learn (*ajar*), and wise (*bijaksana*) in modern Indonesian all derive from Sanskrit—alongside thousands of others. And up until now, the Burmese, Mon, Thai, Khmer, and Lao languages, as well as Javanese, are all written in an India-derived (Brahmic) script.

This great wave of Indianization encompassed almost all of Southeast Asia, as far east as the central coast of Vietnam, where the Chams lived, and into the islands of the Philippine archipelago, where the impact was weakest. Here there were no great monuments or, as far as we know, great mandala kingdoms of the kind that waxed and waned on the mainland and on Java. Even so, in pre-Spanish times, Filipino vernacular languages were written in an India-derived script called *baybayin*, and archaeologists continue to find Hindu- and Buddhist-inspired figures in Philippine digs. (These include a *c.* eleventh-century statuette of the bodhisattva Tara in brilliant gold found in Agusan, Mindanao.)

New waves of Islam and Theravada Buddhism

The Hindu-Buddhist layer of Southeast Asian civilizations was pervasive and has been tenacious. But beginning around 1300, new waves of cultural influence again swept through the region bringing Islam and its message. Islam also came by way of India, where a Muslim dynasty gained dominance after the 1100s, although some of its earliest emissaries to Southeast Asia appear to have traveled directly from the Muslim heartland in Arabia and the Middle East. As with the older Indian influences, no army of foreign invaders carried Islam to Southeast Asia. Instead, Islam was brought peacefully by devout merchants plying the waters between India and Southeast Asia and the traveling scholars and Sufi mystics who arrived in their vessels and rooted themselves in the region's harbor towns and maritime mini-states. Again, the process took many centuries, but by the mid-1400s the ruler of the Straits-controlling mandala at Melaka had converted to Islam and become Sultan Muhammad Shah. Islam's position in the islands accelerated after that as Islam-centered mandalas defeated and incorporated others. By 1500 a Muslim sultan had seized power at Demak on Java.

Islam was soon the hegemonic religious culture in much of the island world, with its influence strongest in coastal maritime kingdoms such as Aceh, Melaka, and Makassar and with is impact attenuating among inland populations, where Hindu-Buddhist legacies were most deeply rooted. Here and there, more or less pure Hindu societies survived amid the widespread adoption of Islam. This was most remarkably true in Bali, which hosted several mini-kingdoms under its own kings, royalty, and priestly castes.

With Islam came the powerful appeal of monotheism and a body of teachings and laws whose sway stretched from Southeast Asia west to the great empires of the Mughals in India, the Safavids in Persia, and others all the way to Africa and Spain. In embracing Islam, its rules and rituals, fasting, almsgiving, and pilgrimage and habits of modesty, Southeast Asians joined a body of believers, or *umma*, that linked them to great centers of knowledge, power, wealth, and piety that spanned the globe, or seemed to.

With Islam also came Arabic, the language of the Qur'an and of Islamic scholarship. As was the case with Sanskrit and Pali, only a handful of religious scholars in Southeast Asia knew the language well. Ordinary Muslims memorized prayers and passages from the Qur'an in Arabic and adopted Arabic words into their vernacular languages, so that today, for example, in Malay and Indonesian, the words for Friday (*jumaat*), news (*kabar*), sincerity (*ikhlas*) and thousands of others are Arabic. (Persian words also arrived with Islam.)

With Islam came the sacred teachings of the Qur'an and the hallowed traditions of the Prophet (Hadith) as well as the popular tales of Sinbad and *A Thousand and One Nights* that also moved effortlessly along Muslim-dominated trade routes. Also, new names arrived. As Muslims, many Southeast Asians began drawing from the huge repository of names in the Qur'an and Hadith and other Muslim societies to become Mahmud, Umar, Abu Bakar, and Ahmad as well as Zubaidah, Chadijah, Laila, and so on.

But not everyone did so, just as not everyone adhered to the new Muslim teachings with the same degree of discipline and devotion. As in earlier borrowings, Southeast Asians adapted Islam selectively and found ways to nest it within older bodies of beliefs and practices. Old calendars, wedding rituals, habits of dress, and naming systems remained alongside the new ones. And despite the strict monotheism of Islam, many Southeast Asian Muslims continued to make offerings to venerated ancient spirits, and they remained wary of, and in awe of, certain spirit-laden sites.

A particularly complex fusion formed in Java, where Islam as commonly practiced clung to certain elements of older Hindu-Buddhist-animist ways in a sort of mystic synthesis. Just as Indianization brought not one monolithic civilization but a dazzling mosaic of Indianized adaptations, so did the spread of Islam. Southeast Asians did not become Arabs any more than Persians, Indians, or North African Muslims did. They became new Muslim versions of themselves.

The deep-to-shallow sway of Islam took in virtually all of the lowland populations of the Indonesian archipelago and Malaya and penetrated the Sulu Sea and islands of the southern Philippine archipelago—a penetration that was arrested by the arrival of the Spanish and Christianity. On the mainland, Muslim enclaves formed along the coasts of the Bay of Bengal and in Champa on the Vietnam coast.

During roughly the same period that Islam overtook the islands, a new school of Buddhism swept through most of the mainland. Theravada Buddhism was a reform movement that sought to purify Buddhist beliefs and practices of superstitions, myths, and embellishments that had occurred over centuries as the religion passed from generation to generation and into cultural landscapes far from its place of origin in India. It sought to return followers to the pure teachings of the Buddha and to a body of austere practices that stood in contrast to the veneration of bodhisattvas, tantric cults, and worship of god-like Buddhas that had proliferated in the expansive Mahayana Buddhist world of East and Southeast Asia. Beginning around the 1000s, Theravada monks bearing Pali-language sutras brought the new teachings to the lowland kingdoms of the Mons and Burmans, the Thai, Khmer, and Lao. To be sure, Burmese *nat*s and Thai *phi* and other local spirits remained and were folded into the new religious regimen.

In this way, Southeast Asia bifurcated into a Buddhist mainland and a Muslim archipelago with a Buddhist-Muslim cusp in the mid-to-lower Malay Peninsula, where the mandalas of the Buddhist Thai overlapped with the mandalas of the Muslim Malays. Thus, whereas the iconic religious architecture of the mainland became the Buddhist monastery, or *wat*, with monks in saffron or red robes, in the islands it became the mosque. Monarchs now presented themselves as patrons of Buddhism on the mainland and, in much of the island world, as righteous defenders of Islam.

China's sway

The centuries-long practice of borrowing from India and the Middle East prevailed everywhere except Vietnam. Here a different Southeast Asian society emerged under the sway of Asia's other great radiating civilization, China. Indeed, the territorial homeland of the Vietnamese along the lower reaches of the Red River and the Red River delta constituted a colony of the Chinese empire for nearly one thousand years under the Han, Sui, Tang, and intervening dynasties. Under a variety of governing arrangements and patterns of ethnic Chinese in-migration and intermarriage, the society that evolved there embraced many features of Chinese civilization and became, one might say, Chinese-like or Sinicized. So deeply embedded were these influences that even after the kingdom of Vietnam (Dai Viet) wrested its independence from the Tang in 939, the Vietnamese elites who assumed power adopted Chinese institutions of government and continued to revere the religious and philosophical systems that they had made their own.

These systems included Mahayana Buddhism, Daoism, and Confucianism—the three elements of Vietnamese (and Chinese) religion. The Confucian values of social hierarchy, in which children defer to parents, wives to husbands, and so on became deeply embedded and underpinned loyalty to the Vietnamese emperor, who ruled Chinese-style as the Son of Heaven and who performed rituals that mimicked those of the emperor of China. Scholar officials modeled on those of China governed the realm in a pattern quite in contrast with officials and regional powers in the Indianized mandala states. And the affluent and literate classes learned the Chinese language and studied the Chinese classics of statecraft, philosophy, and poetry—indeed, as in China, prospective scholar officials were examined competitively on these subjects to qualify for officialdom.

The Vietnamese possessed a language of their own, but it became one filled with Chinese words; in addition, for many centuries until the modern era it was rendered in Chinese characters. (Just as, for example, Malay was rendered in Arabic letters.) In a process of cultural radiation similar to Southeast Asian Indianized societies, Chinese stories became Vietnamese stories, with a familiar cast of characters. Alongside everyday Buddhist practices, including the veneration of Bodhisattva Kuanyin and Daoist lore, the popular culture of China penetrated the popular culture of the Vietnamese—mingling there with stories and arts and spirits of purely local origins. Indeed, local Vietnamese guardian spirits were among those honored with titles and imperial appointments under the emperor.

Despite the apparent coherence of the Chinese model, the Vietnamese Confucian state was in many ways aspirational and subject to the same forces that underlay the political instability of the mandala world. Periods of fragmentation alternated with periods of consolidation. Regional lords and their clans tested the authority of the Son of Heaven and sometimes usurped central power altogether. There were succession disputes, rebellions, and restive non-Vietnamese hill peoples to be appeased and quieted, not to mention aggressive neighbors such as the Chams. As the Vietnamese expanded southward in the 1400s and subsequent centuries, gradually marginalizing the Chams and penetrating the outer rings of the Khmer mandala in the Mekong Delta, they brought new populations under the sway of their strong culture. This created new fusions of a very Southeast Asian kind.

Even after 939, the Vietnamese had China to contend with. On two major occasions, in 1075–1076 under the new Song dynasty and later under the Mongols (1250 and again in 1278), armies from China invaded Vietnam with the intent of bringing this outlying "province" back into the fold. Vietnam's successful resistance created heroes to be long remembered.

Aside from its legacy in Vietnam, China also intervened periodically in the small non-Chinese border states on the southern tier of their empire—locales that today straddle the Yunnan–Southeast Asia border—that were also linked, mandala fashion, to larger Southeast Asian polities of the Burmans, Thai, and Lao on the mainland. Trade networks, language, and shared customs reinforced their inclinations toward Southeast Asia. In Muong Mau, Muong Laem, Muong Lau, and Sipsongpanna (Xishuangbanna), Chinese dynasties occasionally imposed frontier military administrations but usually ruled the region through elite intermediaries or local lords whose power flowed from their status and followings in their immediate domains. Like cunning mandala operators elsewhere, these men of prowess appear to have bent to China at some times and to neighboring Southeast Asian powers at others, all the while keeping advantageous channels of trade open on both sides.

Aside from these cusp societies, and the anomalous invasion attempts by the Mongols (Yuan dynasty), China did not intervene directly in the mandala world of Southeast Asia. Instead, it managed its relationships with the region's multitude of non-Chinese states through the tributary system. Under the tributary system, rulers of barbarian states—from the vantage point of the civilized Middle Kingdom—were invited to pay their respects to the Chinese emperor by sending embassies bearing gifts. These deferential acts would be reciprocated with more valuable gifts in return. This was, in fact, a form of trade that benefited both parties. Yet as a ritual, the tributary system allowed Southeast Asia's beleaguered mandala kings to claim China as a patron. At one time or another, many did so, including Vietnam, Srivijaya, Melaka, Ayutthaya, Majapahit, Champa, Brunei, and Luzon and even small states such as the tiny gold-rich kingdom of Butuan in Mindanao.

It might have been otherwise. In the early 1400s, as the new Ming dynasty (1368–1644) was flexing its muscles, Emperor Yongle (r. 1402–1424) repeatedly sent huge fleets of massive Chinese ships to Southeast Asia (and well beyond) under the command of Zheng He. In Java, Sumatra, Siam, and Melaka the message was electrifying. Nothing remotely as impressive existed in the region. Zheng He and his retinue collected tribute and established local communities of Chinese merchants and shipbuilders, traded in local products, suppressed pirates, and projected Chinese power. China's support helped establish Melaka as a new commerce-driven mandala center on the Straits.

A new era of engagement was at hand, or so it seemed. But in 1433, a new Chinese emperor canceled the project and placed the Chinese Empire behind a barrier of official isolation that lasted for the next several hundred years (during which, significantly, Chinese merchants based along the empire's southern coast continued to trade privately in Southeast Asia).

Southeast Asia on the verge

China's official withdrawal paved the way for Europe, whose first emissaries began arriving in Southeast Asia in the early 1500s. The mandala world they entered hosted hundreds of small kingdoms and a few large ones. Major states waxed and waned in the predictable verdant spots where fertile river plains facilitated large populations of settled rice growers. Along the Irrawaddy, the post-Pagan mandala center at Ava was rapidly waning in the face of competition from rival mandalas to the south (the Mons) and west (in Rakhine) and of restless vassals among the Shans and others along the Yunnan frontier to the north; by 1527 its capital had fallen. In contrast, in Siam along the Chao Phraya, Ayutthaya was waxing strong as its mandala expanded at the expense of weaker neighbors and engaging dynamically in international trade from its cosmopolitan capital. On Ayutthaya's periphery existed smaller mandala kingdoms based at Chiangmai (La Na) and Luang Prabang (Lan Sang). Khmer kings in the lower Mekong held sway over a much-reduced mandala, a remnant of the former Angkor Empire and one that found itself beleaguered by aggressive neighbors. One of these was Vietnam, also waxing strong and recently victorious over its adversarial neighbors to the south, the Chams, whose capital the Vietnamese seized in 1471.

In the island world, aside from Java, the great maritime mandala of Melaka dominated the zone of the Melaka Straits, including the small riverine kingdoms of Malaya as well as coastal Sumatra and Borneo. Aceh, Makassar, Brunei, Patani, and Bantam hosted powerful small states with mandala-like satellites of their own, outside of which smaller harbor-town, riverine, and island polities prevailed; indeed, they proliferated by the hundreds throughout the Indonesian and Philippine archipelagos. In eastern Indonesia, Ternate and Tidore dominated, and in the Philippine archipelago, small mandala-like thalassocracies orchestrated trade linking Chinese merchants to Southeast Asian maritime networks from bases in Manila and Sulu.

Although the core mainland states exhibited a certain level of coherence and permanence, despite more or less constant turbulence in the outer rings of their mandalas, as a whole, the system was inherently unstable. For the Europeans who began arriving in the region in the 1500s, this made establishing a foothold a relatively easy matter.

The arrival of Europeans speaks to yet another aspect of the times: economically, Southeast Asia was dynamic. Beginning around 1400, the region benefited from a confluence of global forces that brought new prosperity to China, India, Europe, and Japan and, in turn, higher levels of trade and prosperity to Southeast Asia. Pepper, cloves, and nutmeg as well as pearls, sandalwood, gems, resins, and delicacies such as birds' nests drove merchants to Southeast Asian ports in ever greater numbers, where they exchanged regional specialties for silks, ceramics, guns, and silver. Silver especially drove the boom as greater and greater quantities arrived in the 1500s from the Spanish Americas and from silver mines in Japan. The new money strengthened mandala centers in both the islands and on the mainland, where states such as Ayutthaya hosted communities of foreign traders at their capitals. Indeed, the region was dotted with emporiums, the richest by far of which was the sultanate of Melaka, whose fame reached far and wide. And so it was that Melaka became the first obvious target when Portuguese conquistadores sailed into the region in 1511 on a mission for gold, God, and glory.

Chapter 3
Colonies

The mandala world of Southeast Asia was fragile, but it was also rich. Merchants from near and far flocked to its markets to gather the region's unique spices such as nutmeg, mace, and cloves as well as black peppercorns, precious woods, resins, and oils. At the major entrepôts such as Melaka, these valuable items were available alongside all the select and commonplace merchandise of Asia, from fine porcelains and silks to everyday tools and pottery. Malay, Bugis, Thai, Filipino, Javanese, and other Southeast Asian merchants managed this trade with great acumen in collaboration and competition with the Indians, Chinese, and Arabs who frequented and often dwelled in the region.

Arab merchants carried Southeast Asian goods to Europe, introducing them into the Mediterranean world, including Venice, through routes that passed through the Persian Gulf and Istanbul. Europeans were drawn to Southeast Asia to gain access to the region's precious goods directly, and in doing so to cut out the Muslims, their great rivals in religion and civilization. The first to do so were the two great Iberian kingdoms of Portugal and Spain, crusading Christian kingdoms that in the 1400s and 1500s roamed the world in their agile sailing ships in search of wealth and glory, both for themselves and for Christendom.

The Portuguese arrived first. Having rounded Africa in 1488, they made quickly for India and Southeast Asia. By 1510 they had established an enclave on the west coast of India at Goa. The following year they captured Melaka, the richest commercial city in Southeast Asia and the center of a powerful Muslim mandala that controlled the Straits. They built a walled city there, with churches and convents, and began acquiring the valuable spices directly at the source in Ambon, Ternate, and Banda.

Spain came from the other side of the world, reaching the Philippine islands from across the Pacific Ocean in Mexico, which they seized from the Aztecs in 1521. In that same year Magellan, a Portuguese explorer sponsored by Spain, reached the islands and claimed them for Spain. (He was subsequently killed there.) After a few further probes, Spain established a permanent beachhead at Manila in 1571 by displacing a local Muslim sultan and building a huge walled city called Intramuros.

For a time Portugal grew rich at home on the basis of its Asia trade far away, which also penetrated China and Japan. Both Portugal and Spain sought to spread the "one true religion" among their subjects and other Asians, namely Roman Catholicism. But whereas Portugal contented itself with a string of commercial outposts and towns—of which Melaka was one of many, including Goa, Ceylon, East Timor, Macao, and Nagasaki—Spanish conquistadores claimed the entire archipelago for their king and named it after him: Las Philipinas. Subsequently, they subjugated all but the southernmost lowland peoples of the Philippines and, in not so long a time, converted them to Christianity, or at least to its outward forms.

The agents of this great cultural transformation were members of religious brotherhoods (Jesuits, Augustinians, Dominicans, Franciscans, and others), missionary monks, or friars, who fanned throughout the islands bearing the Christian doctrine in vernacular languages, building magnificent churches, and also acting as the eyes and ears of Spain's imperial officialdom. In the ensuing centuries, Spain strove to resettle lowland Filipinos within the sound of the church bells and to build church-centered urban communities throughout the islands, complete with plazas, civic buildings, and the homes of local notables—in most cases the descendants of former datus and their families, leading clans of pre-Spanish days who remained elite and influential under the Spanish as Catholic Indios, or Natives.

The friars and other Spaniards grabbed much of the best land for themselves but they also brought to the islands the civilization of Europe. They established schools and universities. (The college that became the University of Santo Tomas was founded in 1611, twenty-five years before Harvard.) And they introduced their language. Only an elite few among Spain's subjects learned Spanish properly, but untold numbers of Spanish words shifted into the vernacular languages of the islands and remain there today. It was also aboard Spanish boats that plied annually between Acapulco and Manila, the famous Manila galleons, that a great many new plants reached Asia from the Americas. These included maize, tobacco, pineapples, potatoes, tomatoes, and chili peppers. (Bananas, papaya, and mangoes sailed the other way.)

Spain's influence was profound but not total. Aside from the friars, very few Spanish people actually lived in the far-flung colony. Most who did tended to cluster in Intramuros at Manila, the center of government and Spanish life with a host of churches, convents, schools, and business houses and the homes of Spanish colonists. A scattering of Spanish officials were posted around the islands—as provincial governors, for example—but most day-to-day administration below the provincial level was carried out by elite Indios who occupied tiers of public offices in districts and towns, where they were chosen by their male peers and vetted by the Spanish priest.

In a pattern already familiar to the region, Filipinos became Christians and celebrated Christmas and Easter and the feast days of their adopted patron saints without wholly abandoning their belief in spirits; ancient spiritual anxieties and practices remained. Spain's reach was also geographically limited. It ended where the hills began and in the southern islands where Islam and a clutch of small mandala-style sultanates were rooted. Hill peoples and Muslims thus remained largely outside the colony's Hispanicizing pull. Still, Las Philipinas was an entirely new entity in Southeast Asia, one with a remarkable legacy.

Portugal's legacy is small by comparison. Although it permanently disrupted Melaka's mandala, it did not establish a landed empire in its place. Instead, it contained its political presence within the enclave itself, which became an essential hub in its operations throughout Asia. Under Portugal, Melaka became a learning and propagation center for Christianity, too. The great Jesuit missionary Francis Xavier was active there. Eventually, however, it was overtaken by aggressive newcomers; the Dutch seized it in 1641. The Portuguese left behind a tiny, neglected outpost in East Timor (until 1975!) and a legacy of cultural artifacts such as Portuguese words (the Malay words for table and shoes, for example), musical instruments, and melodic tunes. Otherwise, they changed Southeast Asia very little.

Arrival of the companies

The Netherlands, however, reshaped the region fundamentally. Its early agents in Southeast Asia were not servants of a crown, as the Portuguese and Spanish had been, but servants of a company, the Dutch East India Company, or VOC as its soon-to-be-global brand identified it. Capitalized in the Low Countries and chartered by the Republic of the United Provinces in 1602, the VOC carried forward Dutch probes into Southeast Asia that had begun in the late 1500s. Like the Iberians before them, the Dutch sought direct access to the region's profitable and unique spices.

The VOC's charter gave it a monopoly of trade in Asia and the authority to wage war, enter into treaties, collect taxes, and occupy

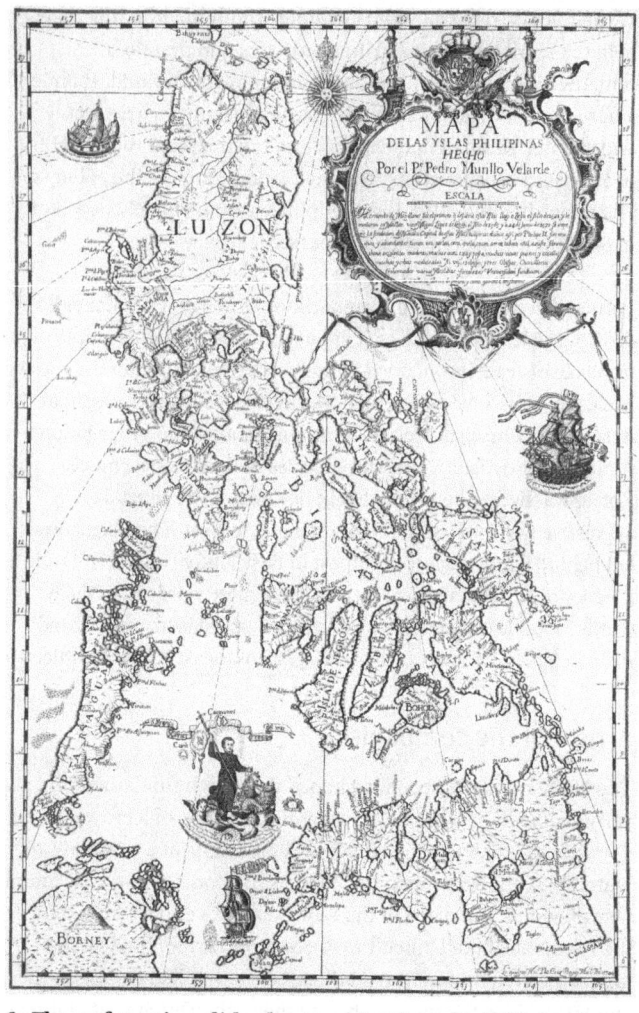

6. The configuration of islands comprising "*las yslas Philipinas*" was new and created wholly by Spain.

and govern territories. The small mandala kingdoms that dotted Southeast Asia's shallow seas became stepping stones for the Dutch as they penetrated the region, port by port. By 1619 they had established a walled-in enclave and hub city on the northwest coast of Java at Jakarta (which they called Batavia). In Maluku, they muscled aside the Portuguese, Spanish, and English to monopolize the nutmeg, mace, and clove trade. The process was savage. In the 1600s, agents of the company expelled or murdered indigenous local producers and confined the production of the spices to certain islands, destroying trees they could not control. In Amsterdam, the value of cloves and other spices soared.

The VOC's hub at Batavia lay on the outer fringes of a great mandala ruled by Sultan Agung, the king of Mataram on Java. Sultan Agung's armies attacked the Dutch entrepôt in 1628 and 1629 but failed to remove it. Instead, in the years and decades to come, the company expanded its presence on the island as the kingdom fell into disorder, peeling off key territories in the outer mandala such as the island's mercantile coastal cities and intervening in succession disputes and other power struggles, often in alliance with local actors. Java's kings were irreparably weakened as their mandalas grew smaller and smaller. By the 1750s the company was utterly dominant. Java's kings and princes had been subordinated to a new Dutch colonial state. The tiny kingdoms of central Java that remained with their royal capitals in Yogyakarta and Surakarta now existed wholly at Dutch discretion.

The Dutch East India Company ruled a vast population of Natives, or Inlanders (as indigenous people were now officially designated). Being parsimonious, it employed only a skeleton staff of white Dutch administrators to manage its colony. Instead, like the Spanish in the nearby Philippines, it incorporated elite local families into its system as administrators. For centuries, Javanese aristocrats, the *priyayi*, had served the island's kings as local lords of the realm, rendering their services and loyalty to kings as determined by the shifting variables of the island's mandalas.

Now, by and large, they served the Dutch; even so, they remained locally prominent and even revered as bearers of Java's high culture and reminders of its rich history.

Unlike elite Filipinos under Spain, the Javanese priyayi did not assimilate to the Dutch religion, nor did Java's common people. The VOC had little interest in promoting Christianity and permitted only a modicum of missionary activity. Nor was it interested in advancing Dutch civilization to Natives. There were no universities in Dutch Java (and no schools of law or engineering until the 1920s). As a result, the dominant culture of Java and its subcultures across the island continued to advance in the deep riverbed already established, in which Islam was the hegemonic religious culture and in which the civilization's Hindu-Buddhist and animist roots endured and evolved.

On the last day of 1799, the Dutch East India Company collapsed under the weight of its accumulated corruption and debts. Its assets and territories were assumed by the Dutch state. By this time, the Netherlands controlled multiple territories in Southeast Asia, including, aside from Java, the spice islands of Maluku and the once-great port city of Melaka. Moreover, its dominant role in maritime trade had subordinated once far-reaching indigenous seafaring traders to the lower tiers of its regional supply chain.

By this time, England had also acquired an entrepôt along the Melaka Straits at Penang, where the sultan of Kedah, a small Malay kingdom, sought protection from the expanding Thai mandala of the nascent Chakri kings to his north by entering into a deal with the English East India Company (EIC) in 1786. The Thais swallowed him up anyway, in 1821, but Penang remained British. Britain also acquired a sleepy outpost at Bengkulu along Sumatra's southwest coast.

In the unstable mandala world of Southeast Asia, Europeans had clear advantages. Europeans had surpassed Asians in matters of shipbuilding, navigation, and mapping. They were propelled by Europe's surging commercial and proto-industrial economy. And their firearms were consistently superior to those of Southeast Asia's many kings (who purchased guns avidly on the emerging global arms market.) More importantly, global empires such as those of Spain and Portugal and the era's huge chartered companies had developed the capacity to mobilize resources and to project power across great distances—a huge advantage even though much could be lost in transmission between Europe and Asia.

To Southeast Asian actors who encountered them on the spot, the links between the officials of the VOC and the English East India Company and the vast matrixes that supported them were invisible, if not incomprehensible. Southeast Asian rulers, large and small, appear to have viewed the Europeans as powerful players acting within the well-understood dynamics of their own mandala world. Depending on the circumstances, they could be either allies or enemies—as in fact, they clearly were with each other.

The establishment of many Western footholds at Melaka, on Java, and in the Philippines opened doors for European newcomers of all nationalities to make their fortunes privately in the region. Southeast Asian rulers engaged with them opportunistically, buying guns and opium from them and enlisting their services as mercenaries and as advisers and intermediaries just as, in earlier centuries, they had welcomed sojourning brahmins and wandering Sufis to their courts. (In seventeenth-century Ayutthaya— to cite a famous example—an enterprising Greek adventurer named Constantine Phaulkon rose to be a titled counselor under King Narai.)

By 1800, the European presence in Southeast Asia was large but far from dominating. Up to this point, Europeans had not yet breached the mainland. Here the kings of the Konbaung and Chakri dynasties were vigorously expanding their mandalas in Burma and Siam. Vietnam was reaching the end of a long civil war and on the brink of a strong new dynasty, the Nguyen, which was proclaimed by Emperor Gia Long in 1802. Smaller mandala kingdoms proliferated on the fringes of these large states (in Cambodia, Laos, and elsewhere along the Yunnan cusp).

In the islands, despite the maritime supremacy of the Netherlands and its domination of Java and the long-evolving hold of Spain over the northern and central islands of the Philippine archipelago, hundreds of small autonomous kingdoms and mini-states dotted the region's sprawling array of land and water. In this complex mosaic, legions of Southeast Asians still lived under the authority of their own indigenous kings while legions of others were evolving in new directions as subjects of European colonies.

Momentum favored the Europeans. Britain had long harbored ambitions in Southeast Asia but had been bested by the VOC in the early 1600s and retreated to India. By the late 1700s, through the agency of the EIC (English East India Company), a chartered company much like the VOC, it had utterly subverted the huge crumbling mandala of India's Mughal dynasty and established hegemonic control over the subcontinent. Its new probes into Southeast Asia led to the temporary occupation of Spanish Manila between 1762 and 1764 and soon yielded the Melaka Straits colony of Penang in 1789, cunningly wrested from the sultan of Kedah. In the following decades the EIC moved aggressively to expand its presence, seizing upon the opportunity of the Napoleonic Wars to grab Java from the Netherlands for four years (1812 to 1816)— returning it after the Congress of Vienna—and subsequently establishing a second Straits entrepôt at Singapore in 1819.

By design, Penang and Singapore attracted large numbers of Chinese migrants, who became the majority populations of these British-run trade hubs. In an 1824 treaty, Britain secured its supremacy over the Melaka Straits by acquiring Melaka itself from the Netherlands, swapping it for its slumbering outpost at

Bengkulu in Sumatra. The Straits now demarcated British and Dutch spheres of influence, that is, territories in which each power would be free to expand without interference from the other. This was a harbinger of things to come.

The nineteenth-century onslaught

By the early twentieth century, the colonial spheres of the Netherlands and Great Britain had expanded dramatically and both France and the United States had also seized colonial territories in Southeast Asia. Indeed, by this time, only one of the region's hundreds of mandala kingdoms had survived. The rest, large and small, had all been subsumed within the vast empires of the world's Western powers. This onslaught unfolded rapidly in the nineteenth century in a process that revealed both the competitive ambitions and the strengths of the West's rising industrial states and the inherent weaknesses of Southeast Asia's mandala kingdoms.

Britain's huge colony in India included Bengal, which lay adjacent to territories that figured in the outer circles of Burma's large mandala—territories into which the armies of the Konbaung kings were expanding violently in the late 1700s and early 1800s. The resulting rebellions and flows of refugees into British territory led to conflicts between the kingdom and the EIC. Burma's kings, flush from recent victories against China, badly underestimated their new foe. Britain's successful invasion by steamship up the Irrawaddy River led to a treaty in 1826 in which King Bagyidaw (r. 1819–1837) lost large portions of his outer mandala (in Tenasserim, Arakan, Manipur, and Assam) and also forced open the kingdom to Western trade and other influences through the Irrawaddy port city of Rangoon.

These events set the stage for further conflicts that resulted again in British invasions, in the 1850s and 1880s. The first resulted in the loss of "lower Burma," the southern half of the kingdom's mandala, and the second in the conquest of the mandala center at Mandalay. By 1886 Britain had abolished the Burmese monarchy, exiled the king and queen, and annexed the territories of the entire kingdom to British India, including many non-Burman territories of groups such as the Shan, Kachin, and Karen.

These episodes of conquest paralleled the penetration of Burma by floods of new capital and enterprises, especially in the Burma delta after Britain seized it in the 1850s; opened it to migrants from northern Burma, India, and China; and introduced its rice to world markets. By 1910, Burma was the largest exporter of rice in the world.

Similar economic forces were in play elsewhere in Britain's "sphere." Its Melaka Straits enclaves at Penang, Melaka, and Singapore—collectively, the Straits Settlements—lay alongside a collection of small Malay Muslim kingdoms on the Malay Peninsula. Before the Portuguese conquest, these river-based sultanates had been part of Melaka's great mandala. Now four of them, including Kedah, formed the lower tier of Siam's huge mandala under the Chakri dynasty. The rest were autonomous under their sultans and many titled nobles and chiefs.

Like most small kingdoms of the mandala world, the Malay states had long engaged in external trade, yielding valuable upriver products such as rattan and resins to markets beyond. And a few, Perak and Selangor in particular, hosted tin mines. Britain's new commerce-driven settlements along the coast became conduits for British investments and migrating Chinese merchants and workers into the kingdoms. As the global demand for tin rose, new capital and technologies were introduced. Mining camps with large numbers of Chinese men mushroomed into frontier boomtowns, where institutions such as secret societies arose to meet pressing social needs and to compete for the profits of labor recruiting, gambling, prostitution, and opium.

These dynamic new forces disrupted the stability of the small Malay kingdoms, several of which fell into disorder as secret society gang wars conflated with succession disputes and other mandala-like power struggles. Eventually, the mayhem spread into the Straits Settlements themselves. In 1874, Britain took action. (The English East India Company had been nationalized in 1858.) Beginning in Perak and subsequently in the other states, Britain seized control of the sultanates (in places, militarily) by placing British "residents" in charge of the territories' worldly management and allocating "religion and customs of the Malays" to the sultans, who now became British clients living in vastly improved palaces.

Although the particulars varied, this was the guiding concept of British Malaya, which by 1909 encompassed all nine of the sultanates, including Kedah and the others that King Chulalongkorn of Siam ceded to Britain in that year. Builders of the British Empire at the time spoke of a civilizing mission. One of them, Frank Swettenham, wrote, "Time means progress and expansion for all that part of Malaya which comes under British influence." Even so, he said, "the Malays are the people of the country." We have made their interests "our first consideration."

As these events transpired in the Malay Peninsula, other British actors carved out colonial territories in northern Borneo. These included the swashbuckling James Brooke, who, beginning in 1841, peeled off one outlying territory after another of the sultan of Brunei's mandala until his own private kingdom, Sarawak, controlled all but a tiny remnant at the capital. In 1888, the much-diminished sultan applied for British "protection." Secure within the sway of the British imperial navy, Brooke and his successors ruled Sarawak as white rajas until World War II.

Meanwhile, in 1881 an agribusiness company chartered in England with interests in timber, copra, and other tropical commodities acquired a vast territory in the northeast of Borneo from both the sultan of Brunei and the sultan of Sulu, each of whom claimed it as part of their overlapping mandalas. The

British North Borneo Company held the territory, now the Malaysian state of Sabah, for fifty-nine years. Thus, Sarawak, North Borneo, and the sultanate of Brunei all came under European sway by the early twentieth century.

During the same years in which Britain advanced upon Burma, Malaya, and nearby territories, the Netherlands moved forth from its stronghold on Java into the rest of the Indonesian archipelago. This staggering undertaking of the nineteenth century involved untold acts of diplomacy, threat, marauding, and outright war during which literally hundreds of small kingdoms were first subordinated to the hegemonic power of the Dutch and finally subjugated altogether. From the Dutch perspective, the autonomous mini-kingdoms of the archipelago—as well as larger and stronger ones in Aceh, Bali, and Makassar—represented territorial loose ends and openings for other European interlopers (such as privateers like James Brooke). As enclaves where contraband guns and opium were traded and where rebels and pirates could find sanctuary, they threatened Dutch *rust en orde* (calm and order).

The Dutch astutely took advantage of the big fish–small fish nature of the mandala world by guaranteeing the territories of this particular raja or that in return for deference and trade monopolies—often specified in long treaties. Mini-kings found this advantageous. Joseph Conrad remarks of one Malay chief of the 1880s (in *Outcast of the Islands*) that he sought to "apply to the Orang Blanda [the Dutch] for a flag, for that protection which would make them safe forever!"

But where sultans and rajas refused to be pliant and where local civil wars and other disruptions threatened, the Dutch were more than willing to go to war. They did so brutally against independent communities of Chinese gold miners in Borneo, against Wahabist Islamic reformers in Sumatra, against the powerful sultanate of Aceh, and, finally, against the two remaining independent kingdoms of Bali, whose kings and noble families, acknowledging defeat, committed ritual suicide as colonial soldiers closed in firing. Eventually, the Dutch replaced all the long treaties with short ones in which once-deferential allies became subjects. By the early twentieth century, the Dutch East Indies was complete, the most massive colony in all Southeast Asia.

As for France, its imperial ambitions had long been in play in the Americas and in India. French missionaries had also been among the first in Asia. One of them, Alexandre de Rhodes, a Jesuit, made early inroads in Vietnam, where in the 1600s he invented a roman letter–based system for writing Vietnamese to replace or complement the use of Chinese characters. In 1658, Rhodes initiated a French missionary society dedicated to proselytizing in Asia. Two centuries later, another French Jesuit, Pigneau de Béhaine, actively aided Nguyen Anh in the civil war that resulted in his elevation to become Emperor Gia Long and founder of the new Nguyen dynasty in 1802. By this time there were some three hundred thousand Vietnamese Catholics.

The growth of Catholicism in the years that followed led to harsh repression by the kingdom's Confucian mandarins and kings, and the action served as the official provocation for French intervention. Gunboat attacks began in 1858, and by 1867 France had established a full-fledged colony in southern Vietnam. Subsequent events revealed the degree to which French imperialists were also motivated by the desire to open Vietnam's commercial ports and to use Vietnam as a gateway to rich markets in China. In a sequence of defeats, Vietnam's kings relinquished the kingdom's sovereignty step by step until, in 1885, following a war in which Chinese armies failed to defend the kingdom, France claimed the entire state. The colony was divided into three parts: Tonkin, Annam, and Cochinchina—all governed somewhat differently. In Annam, a Nguyen puppet monarch remained. But there was no question: Vietnam was a French colony.

Meanwhile, in 1863, King Norodom of Cambodia, witnessing French victories in nearby Vietnam (his mandala enemy to the east) and facing encroachments by Siam (his mandala enemy to the west), placed his beleaguered kingdom under French protection. Likewise, in 1893, the princes of a cluster of tiny Lao polities caught in the mandala cusp between Siam and Vietnam were also persuaded to join Cambodia and Vietnam as constituent members of French Indochina.

By the 1890s, the Philippines had evolved under Spanish rule for three centuries. A mature Hispanicized society had formed, and within it a passionate anti-Spanish anger among some members of the colony's elite intelligentsia and urban dwellers. The revolution they launched in 1896 was the first of its kind anywhere in Southeast Asia. After it foundered, an improbable sequence of events involving Cuba drew the United States to the islands. In an imperial conflict with Spain, the United States at first embraced and then betrayed the Filipino republican revolutionaries and seized the Philippines for itself. When Filipinos resisted, another brutal colonial conquest followed and the United States became the final Western power to claim a vast body of Southeast Asian subjects.

The colonies of Southeast Asia were complete. Of the region's indigenous kingdoms, only Siam survived. This remarkable feat was the consequence of astute leadership. In many ways, the Chakri kings were classical mandala monarchs. They rose to power following the defeat by Burma of the former Thai dynasty at Ayutthaya. Having established a new capital at Bangkok, the Chakris advanced aggressively upon the outer fringes of the kingdom, claiming large numbers of subjects under their sway. These included Lao princes to the northeast, hill peoples in the uplands of the north, Khmer territories in Siem Reap and Battambang, and the four Malay kingdoms of Kedah, Perlis, Kelantan, and Trengannu in the far south. They differed, however, in their response to the European threat.

Rama IV, or Mongkut (1851–1868), was a well-educated polymath who studied Latin and English. He befriended Westerners who arrived in Bangkok and learned from them. He read newspapers from the British Straits Settlements. He knew what was happening in Burma and other parts of the region. By the time he became king in 1851 he was better prepared than any other Southeast Asian king to grasp the nature of the dangers his kingdom faced. Instead of resisting the demands of the West, he made deft concessions to Westerners, beginning with the British in 1855. When they asked to trade freely in the kingdom, he granted it. When they insisted on importing opium, he agreed. An ambassador in the capital? Extraterritorial rights for British subjects? Agreed and agreed. And so on. Mongkut granted the same rights to a queue of other powers, too.

Meanwhile, Mongkut and his son and successor Rama V, Chulalongkorn (1868–1910), made sure that Siam did not descend into the kind of disorder that encouraged foreigners to intervene, discerning astutely that Britain and France, the European powers advancing on the mainland, might find it useful to maintain a stable buffer between their zones of expansion in Burma and Indochina. Father and son embarked on an all-out project of self-strengthening, bringing in a slew of Western advisers, adopting Western models of governance, and educating young Thai elites, including their own children, in Western languages and knowledge. As the Thai state grew stronger, its mandala grew smaller. Chulalongkorn bowed to imperial pressures and ceded territories to France in Laos and Cambodia and to Britain in Malaya. But the kingdom itself survived, even as its rulers transformed it to resemble the Western colonial states that dominated the rest of the region. Thai monarchs were not unique among Southeast Asian kings in executing self-strengthening strategies to stave off the West. They were unique in succeeding.

High colonialism in Southeast Asia

By the late nineteenth century, Southeast Asia was no longer a mosaic of colonial territories and mandalas. Aside from Siam, Western colonies wholly dominated the region. It was a period of almost total white supremacy. As political projections from Europe and the United States, the Southeast Asian colonies illustrated Karl Marx's 1848 prediction in the *Communist Manifesto* that the Western bourgeoisie would "create a world after its own image." In this the Western colonies did not utterly succeed. But they changed Southeast Asia profoundly.

Colonial states such as the Dutch East Indies, British Burma, and the American Philippines were not mandala states. Their borders were fixed on maps, surveyed, and monitored. In the islands, the British and Dutch marked their coastlines with lighthouses and patrolled them with marine police. Colonial administrators endeavored to fill in the state's once-vague edges with an apparatus of power so that, now, there actually was a place—a line—at which the authority of one colony stopped and that of another one began. In practice, these borders were notoriously porous where smuggling, trafficking, and migration was concerned. But they were understood to exist and to demarcate fully bounded states. This included Siam, too, as one of the many adjustments to life in a neighborhood of European powers entailed fixing its borders.

These new states were governed, at the senior level, by white officials sent from Europe and employed in increasingly specialized bureaucracies. The most senior official was ordinarily a governor-general who, following the collapse of the East India companies, reported to a senior minister at home, usually a minister of colonies (but in the United States the secretary of war). These ministers reported, in turn, to their prime ministers and were also called upon to testify before parliament or congress, one of the great ironies of the era being that the colonial powers of Southeast Asia were all democracies.

Metropolitan control also determined the nature of the colonial states' relationships to each other. In the mandala world, neighbors were enemies. In the colonial world the relationship between, say,

British Malaya and the Dutch East Indies was fixed in Europe. If Britain and the Netherlands were on good terms at home, they also strove to cooperate in Southeast Asia, despite aggressive economic competition.

Generally speaking, colonial policies were established in the metropolitan centers and executed in the colonies. Great debates occurred on colonial issues in London, Paris, and the Hague. In fact, however, white colonial officials located on the ground in Southeast Asia were powerful. The governor-general of the Dutch East Indies ruled a territory forty-three times larger than the Netherlands itself. Provincial governors and district officers often had omnibus responsibilities for governing large numbers of subjects and for supervising the projects of the colonial state.

This was possible because beneath the top—the white tiers of colonial administrations—stood tiers and tiers of Southeast Asians who performed the day-to-day work of governance. They included district-level administrators recruited from indigenous elites and aristocracies as well as tax collectors and police and office clerks and, in the twentieth century, modern specialists such as surveyors, paramedics, foresters, and school teachers. With rare exceptions, only the officers of colonial armies were British, French, Dutch, and American (or other European ethnicity); the rank and file were generally made up of Native minorities.

In the colonies small white heads rested upon large Native bodies. This explains how such a small number of Europeans and Americans managed to dominate and govern Southeast Asian populations so much larger than their own numbers. In the Dutch East Indies at the peak of Dutch power in 1930, there were 250 Natives for every European (a census category that included Eurasians, Turks, Filipinos, and Japanese). In French Indochina the figure was 665. The superiority of whites was often fixed in colonial law codes and was universally understood. The protocols of colonial social life made this clear as retinues of Southeast Asian servants now served in white households as nannies, cooks, sweepers, launderers, gardeners, and drivers. In the rijsttafel (rice table smorgasbord) of Dutch Java, a dozen Native waiters stood in line to serve a single white diner.

In the early centuries of European and Southeast Asian interaction, intermarriage across status and color lines was common; in places, large and prominent mestizo clans emerged. But in the age of high colonialism in the late nineteenth and early twentieth centuries, children of mixed race made for awkward accommodations. Depending upon the status and legal initiatives of the parents, some were elevated into the ruling class, others became Natives. In mature colonies, stable social categories formed in which Eurasians were explicitly identified, as in the Spanish mestizos of the Philippines. Among the "pure" whites, demeaning stigmas usually applied. (Anxieties surrounding persons of mixed race are frequently depicted in stories of the times by Western authors such as George Orwell, Somerset Maugham, Louis Couperus, and Marguerite Duras.)

7. In the rijsttafel of Dutch Java, a dozen Native waiters stood in line to serve a single white diner. As a contemporary Jakarta advertisement reveals, these days everyone is welcome to enjoy the rijsttafel.

One of the great underlying purposes of the high colonial states was to draw an ever-escalating quantity of Southeast Asian resources to the West's hungry economies. The colonial states and Western capitalists took advantage of their overwhelming power to develop the region as a major global base of industrial-scale agribusiness and resource extraction. The Dutch began exporting large quantities of coffee, tea, and sugar after 1830 through a state-led system of forced cultivation. By the late nineteenth century, however, private plantations were the norm. Everywhere in Southeast Asia great swaths of land were opened to grow coffee, tea, and sugar as well as tobacco, palm oil, abaca, and rubber. Southeast Asians became menial wage laborers as plantation workers—planting, tending, and tapping rubber trees; picking tea leaves; cutting cane and working under the eyes of white European overseers and ultimately for large agribusiness companies such as Michelin (rubber), Dole (fruits), and Schimmelpenninck (tobacco).

In the Philippines, great sugar haciendas arose in Luzon and the Visayas. Mining companies flourished throughout the colonial world, yielding Malayan tin, Philippine gold, Vietnamese coal, and Burmese gems to global markets alongside petroleum from Burma, Sumatra, and Borneo. Royal Dutch Shell dominated oil production in the Dutch East Indies. Facilitating the movement of these commodities were new steamship lines, roads and railroads, and harbors. At the intersections of the new traffic patterns linking commodities to markets appeared bustling new towns, hubs of dynamic exchange that attracted merchants, artisans, and workers of all kinds. At the same time, the region's larger cities blossomed into major international trade hubs and colonial administrative centers, spreading beyond their historical cores into new suburbs and satellite towns: Manila, Saigon, Singapore, Batavia, Rangoon.

Populations soared during the period, and they also spread out. Responding to the opportunities and pressures of the colonial economies, indigenous Southeast Asians shifted to the new plantation zones for wage work, sometimes as indentured laborers. (Slavery was now forbidden in the colonies and also in Siam.) They also swept out of population-pressed home territories into large fertile spaces of as-yet-unopened land in places such as the southern delta lands of Burma and Vietnam and the Luzon plains, to grow wet rice for the market. Many prospered as farmers and cash-crop producers and also learned the hard lessons of the global economy when commodity prices plummeted.

As the region's remaining forests and swamps were cleared to make way for plantations and homesteading farmers, and as the land filled with people, primordial ecological equations began to shift, a process exacerbated by logging and mining in the forested hills. Animal and plant habitats diminished. By the end of the colonial era, Southeast Asia's environment had been almost wholly reshaped by humans.

Newcomers from China

Southeast Asia's age of colonies also brought legions of newcomers from China. Chinese merchants had traversed the region for centuries, and permanent settlements of Chinese had long existed in many Southeast Asian cities. But now the numbers increased dramatically. Pushed by dearth and disorder in China and pulled by Southeast Asia's burgeoning colonial economy, poor Chinese men by the hundreds of thousands fled China to find work and opportunity in the British, French, Dutch, and Spanish/American colonies—indeed everywhere in the region, including Thailand.

Many Chinese men came as menial coolies and did the dirty work of tin and gold mining, of lifting and loading at the wharves, and of sweeping and cleaning. Others found work in the businesses of already established Chinese migrants and became tinkers and tailors and carpenters and itinerant peddlers of consumer merchandise. Some started multipurpose shops and began to collect the local vegetables, fruits, and eggs of local farmers in exchange for credit to buy seeds, tools, carts, and draft animals. Chinese shops like these proliferated.

In time, small Chinese businesses became larger Chinese businesses. Carpenters and masons became contractors. Shopkeepers became moneylenders and bankers. Entrepreneurs became tycoons. By the early twentieth century, every colony had produced Chinese businessmen of immense fortune and influence. More significantly, in virtually every colony the Chinese had come to occupy the essential urban middle echelons of the regional economies. From whom could you buy a pair of scissors, mops, watering cans, pots, and pans? Gold and silver jewelry? A time piece, a bicycle, a water pump? Who could organize a work crew to move cane from the fields to the mill? To build a house? A church? To whom could you sell surplus rice, eggs, and fruit or rattan, resins, and honey collected from the forest? In most places and cases, by the early twentieth century in Southeast Asia, the answers to these questions involved someone of Chinese descent.

8. In the age of colonies, hundreds of thousands of men fled China to find opportunity in Southeast Asia. Migrants such as these pose for a photograph around 1890 in Dutch Borneo.

The impact of these migrations from China was uneven. Far greater numbers, relative to local populations, amassed in British Penang and Singapore and in the British Malay States, where the Chinese population rose to half the total and more. But all Southeast Asian cities now had substantial Chinatowns and the colonies and Thailand had large numbers of Chinese residents, from 2 to 4 percent in the Dutch East Indies and French Indochina to 10 to 12 percent in Thailand and the Philippines. Burma was an exception in the sense that it also drew large numbers of migrants from India, as did Malaya, Penang, and Singapore to a lesser degree.

The European regimes in Southeast Asia found the hardworking, money-savvy Chinese useful. Until the late nineteenth century, the British, Dutch, and French relied on them as revenue farmers who paid for the privilege of selling opium and collecting tolls. But they feared them, too. In most colonies Chinese were forbidden to buy agricultural land and confined to urban areas and urban occupations. There were periodic crackdowns (and in earlier centuries anti-Chinese massacres in Manila and Batavia). As the numbers of Chinese rose, so did talk of the Yellow Peril. For indigenous Southeast Asians the Chinese were also problematic. As suppliers of goods and credit, they were welcome; but as debt collectors and marketplace tricksters (a common stereotype), they were mistrusted and despised. The king of Siam, Vajiravudh, Chulalongkorn's Oxford-educated son, famously published an anti-Chinese pamphlet in 1914. Despite some intermarriage and assimilation, this ambivalence became rooted in Southeast Asia's new plural societies as they evolved toward the present.

New borrowings

These powerful changes in the economy, demography, and social composition of Southeast Asia during the age of colonies was accompanied by equally profound cultural changes. In a new wave of borrowing and adapting that mirrored the earlier periods of

Indianization and Islamization, Southeast Asians now encountered, and selectively embraced, the West.

White colonizers disagreed about whether it was a good idea to educate Natives as Westerners. The civilizing mission—creating a world after the West's own image—was complicated by racism. The idea, for example, of Burmese and Indonesians and Vietnamese mimicking the British, French, and Dutch was not all that attractive to many colonial whites. In most Southeast Asian colonies, Western education, that is, education in Western languages following a Western school curriculum, was strictly limited to Native elites and certain other well-to-do subjects. Some schools were designed to train Native officials in Western bureaucratic practices. For everyone else, the regimes offered a modicum of vernacular-language primary education, the quality and availability of which varied widely. (In British Burma in the 1920s only 4 percent of Native children advanced beyond grade four.) In places, missionary schools offered an alternative to this pattern. In the Philippines, American colonizers applied models of "industrial education" designed for racial minorities (e.g., at the Tuskegee Institute in Alabama) and introduced English-language education at a popular level, although in practice not universally.

Generally speaking, only a tiny handful of Southeast Asians were offered Western educations, and fewer still, university or professional-level degrees. As the colonial era matured, the Western regimes opened new slightly more advanced schools for health workers, surveyors, and teachers. Graduates of these schools formed the basis of a nascent professional middle class, part of a rising tide of people literate in the vernacular languages and the region's first true generation of readers.

As a small few learned English, French, and Dutch, words from these languages flooded into Southeast Asian vernacular languages, just as Sanskrit, Arabic, and Chinese words had done in earlier periods. English words now punctuated colloquial

Burmese, Malay, and Tagalog. French words became Vietnamese words. In the Dutch East Indies, people now went to the *bioskoop* and enjoyed *pikus-nikus* and *dansa-dansi*. They took photographs with a *kodak* and used Dutch words for car parts such as clutch, gears, and mufflers. (They still do.) Filipinos put food in the "fridge."

It was largely through the vernacular-language press that Southeast Asians learned of the wider world. Newspapers and magazines catering to the region's rising class of literates featured stories from the world round—revolution in China, war in Europe, radical reforms in Muslim Turkey under Kemal Atatürk. Southeast Asians read Western books in translation (*The Three Musketeers!*) and avidly watched European and American movies. Western popular music also swept into the region and already in the 1920s and 1930s there were local Southeast Asian versions of Western band music and jazz.

Likewise, urban Southeast Asian men began wearing jackets and trousers and Panama hats; women adopted skirts and dresses and coiffed their hair Hollywood-style and tried lipstick and rouge. Despite some disapproval, this was true of many urban Southeast Asians and their elites and also of the region's now-large population of Chinese. Family photographs of the period document these changes vividly.

More profoundly, both through the elite Western-language educations of the few and the mass vernacular learning of the many, a body of new ideas entered Southeast Asia. These included the fundamentals of Western science, geography, and economics; popular theories, including social Darwinism; and biographies of historical figures such as George Washington. By the 1920s, new political ideas such as democracy, socialism, and communism were the subjects of passionate popular discussion, debate, and action. The civilizing mission of colonialism thus bore within it the seeds of its own destruction.

The high point of Western colonialism occurred in the early twentieth century. This is when Western rule seemed permanently secure. (Keep in mind that Asia's own great radiating civilizations were both deeply compromised at the time—India as a colony of Britain and China undergoing a tumultuous political revolution.) But World War I weakened the Western powers and new political ideas and movements began to undermine their empires from the inside. By the 1930s, all of Asia and Southeast Asia was astir with nationalism.

The colonial powers reacted differently. Britain, faced with a sophisticated nationalist movement in India, yielded to nationalists in Burma by granting a high degree of home rule that involved an elected Burmese government and prime minister by the late 1930s. The United States also promised home rule in the Philippines. Under the Commonwealth of the Philippines of 1935, Filipinos wrote their own constitution and elected the entire national government and a president.

France and the Netherlands were much less willing to ease their colonies toward home rule. Despite permitting certain elected councils and elite collaborative bodies, they found it harder to consider the end of empire. In 1931, Bonifacius Cornelis de Jonge, governor-general of the Dutch East Indies, predicted confidently that the Netherlands would remain in the Indies for another three hundred years. The following year, Pierre Pasquier, governor-general of French Indochina, predicted that, in Vietnam, France could look forward to "the flowering and the expansion of one of the most beautiful branches that has sprouted from her genius."

However, nationalism and Japanese imperial armies changed everything. And sooner than anyone expected, Southeast Asia's colonies became nations.

Chapter 4
Nations

Most of Southeast Asia's colonies had been created by conquest and coercion. European rule was not welcome. Almost everywhere, Southeast Asians attempted to fend it off in every way possible. The sultan of Melaka rallied allies from neighboring states to drive away the Portuguese. Sultan Agung launched huge assaults against the Dutch fortress at Batavia. Burmese and Vietnamese kings went to war to save their kingdoms from the British and the French. And so it went across the region in encounters large and small.

The odds were against them, given the overpowering edge possessed by Europeans in weaponry and the logistics of wielding power. Even so, the sultanate of Aceh kept the Dutch at bay for thirty years. And elsewhere violent resistance made colonial conquests expensive and painful for advancing Westerners. (Referring to the British conquest of Burma, Kipling wrote of "the dead beneath our awnings...on the road to Mandalay.") When the dust settled and subjugation became a fact of life, memories of heroic resistance fueled the popular imagination and kept alive the dream of freedom.

Being colonized was a humiliation. It subjugated Southeast Asians to laws, regulations, and institutions of authority that were foreign. It relegated elites to second-class status in the colonial social hierarchy and to subordinate places in colonial bureaucracies. It rendered kings throneless or converted them into puppets who reigned in splendor but who had no power to rule.

Colonialism was also an insult to the region's religions. The builders of the British Empire in Burma nonchalantly entered Buddhist shrines with their shoes on and belittled the *sangha*, or monkhood. Muslims felt rage and humiliation under the thumb of the Dutch—nonbelievers for whom Islam was a medieval religion worthy of scorn.

Being colonized also interfered with the routines and customs of ordinary men and women. Colonial tax collectors pressed upon scarce resources, imposed new fines and fees, and interfered with traditional patron-client practices that had softened the burden of rents and taxes in lean years. New rules and regulations also limited people's access to traditional sources of sustenance, including forests and other commons that colonial governments claimed as state land.

For all of these reasons, resistance and rebellion were constant phenomena in the colonial world. Peasants rose against colonial tax collectors and their Native agents. Religious and cult leaders led bands of followers against infidel officials. And members of the nobility and upper classes struggled to restore their kings and princes to power. At times, all of these elements were in play simultaneously. These outbursts kept colonial regimes on edge but inevitably failed in the face of overwhelming force. Even so, they kept alive a spirit of resistance. Their leaders became figures of lore.

Embracing nationalism

In time, a new form of resistance emerged. It grew first among the new classes of Western-educated Southeast Asians, the young Filipinos, Indonesians, Vietnamese, and Burmese who spoke

Spanish, Dutch, French, and English. For this small group, education led to agency. From among their ranks arose the first generation of modern Southeast Asian men and women of prowess. Their educations and experience exposed them to Western Enlightenment ideas of reason and science, to the concepts of liberty and democracy, and to the revolutionary appeals of the American and French Revolutions and of Karl Marx. They became reformers and critics of the colonial state. They came to discern the difference between the kingdoms of the past and the modern nations of the West. And they began, some of them, to visualize their own colonized societies as nations-in-the-making. Hence they became *nationalists*.

This new concept was based not on the mandala states of old or of legitimacy borne of religious authority or, as in Vietnam, of a classical patrimonial Asian philosophy, but upon the notion of legitimacy residing within a body of citizens. And who, exactly, would these citizens be? None other than the subjects of the colonies. What would constitute the territories and boundaries of the new nations? The answer: They would be exactly co-terminus with those of the colonies. The new nation of Burma, for example, would embrace all the territory claimed by Britain as part of British Burma; Indonesia, the name chosen in the early twentieth century to convey the idea of a nation born within the Dutch East Indies, would be the same size and shape as the Indies itself. And so on. Colonies would become nations. And Natives would be citizens.

This was a fine dream, but given the strength of the colonial states, how could it be achieved? Beginning in the first decades of the twentieth century, Western-educated Southeast Asians began to organize movements for political reform and independence. Southeast Asia's proto-nationalists were a varied lot. Some were cautious and concentrated their efforts on self-strengthening—on improving themselves as better Buddhists and Muslims or on defending the positions of certain beleaguered groups, such as

Java's aristocratic priyayi. They founded clubs and schools and published journals. Others complained loudly, agitated, and became openly revolutionary. Some organized movements centered on religion. Others harkened to the example of Asian nationalists such as Mohandas K. Gandhi in India, Sun Yatsen in China, or the Meiji-era nation builders in Japan. And some became communists. Asia's first Communist Party was formed in 1920 in the Dutch East Indies, a year before such a party was founded in China. Indeed, for Southeast Asians, colonialism inadvertently ushered in a new era of protean possibilities.

A few examples will illustrate the complexity of the process. In Burma, the first acts of resistance occurred in the immediate wake of the British seizure of Mandalay in 1885, where royal officials and Buddhist monks mobilized armed support in a failed attempt to restore the king and the old order. (It took several years for Britain to quell the resistance.) By 1906, a group of English-educated students had organized the Young Men's Buddhist Association, the YMBA, whose self-improving members agitated for reforms, not rebellion. They protested against shoe-wearing in Buddhist shrines, colonial schools that promoted Western values, and Burma's colonial identification as a province of British India.

As Britain opened Burma to incremental home rule in the 1920s, many elite Western-educated young people entered public life as members of advisory and legislative councils and, eventually, by the late 1930s, a full-fledged elected Burmese government. (In step with these changes, Britain finally separated Burma from India in 1937.) An English- and French-educated lawyer, Ba Maw, was elected prime minister. Political actors like Ba Maw were passionate nationalists but nationalists who chose to advance their cause incrementally within the colonial state, agitating for new doors to be opened and, when they opened, walking through them. This was a common pattern in other colonies, too. But in Burma and elsewhere, more revolutionary forces were also in play.

By the time Ba Maw became prime minister in 1937, Britain's colony in Burma had been rocked profoundly by the global depression, which rendered many of its once-prosperous small farmers landless and which led to deadly interethnic riots targeting moneylenders from India and other foreigners. Amid troubling stirrings like these, in 1930 a large millenarian rebellion surfaced in which politicized peasants and nascent urbanites rose against the colonial state in an attempt to reestablish the "kingdom of Burma." The rebellion's charismatic leader and would-be king, Shaya San, was captured by the British, defended in the colonial courts by Ba Maw, and hanged. As these alarming events brought the harsh underlying realities of British Burma to light, a new generation of elite nationalists turned in a radical direction. Under Aung San, the We Burmans Society, or Thakins, declared themselves socialists, spurned Ba Maw and other collaborating gradualists, and organized for revolution.

Just as Buddhism provided a public identity around which Burmese opponents of Britain could rally, in Indonesia Islam became a rallying call. Among the earliest politicized movements in the Dutch East Indies were Muhammadiyah (the way of Muhammad) and Sarekat Islam (Islamic Union), both launched in 1912. Whereas Muhammadiyah focused on Muslim self-strengthening through education, community organizing, and the propagation of a stream of reform-minded Islam that embraced modernity, Sarekat Islam took a more agitational approach and stirred the anti-Dutch feelings of its followers. It boasted two million members by 1919. One of its branches, influenced by Dutch socialists on the spot (including an early Comintern agent), declared itself a Communist Party in 1920.

It was about this time that the word *Indonesia* was gaining currency as the name of the colony's nation-to-be. "Indonesia" became a beacon for a proliferating number of nationalist and proto-nationalist groups. In 1928, following a failed uprising by the young Communists, a congress of elite young nationalists pledged themselves, in the Youths' Oath, to Indonesia: one country, one nation, one language. Wholly in sync with this spirit, a young Dutch-educated engineer named Sukarno proposed that nationalism itself could bring together the colony's diverse peoples, religions, and ideologies, including Islam and communism. Sukarno's proactive stand of noncooperation was further than many of the colony's activists wanted to go, and it provoked the Dutch, who arrested him and kept him out of circulation for years, along with many of his like-minded colleagues. Nevertheless, by the 1930s, the dream of a free Indonesia animated the hopes of virtually all the colony's politicized organizations, revolutionary or not.

Opposition to the French in Vietnam was vociferous from the beginning. In the early twentieth century, Phan Boi Chau was already conspiring for revolution on the models of Meiji Japan and Sun Yatsen in China. Chau failed but inspired others. By the 1920s, the colony supported several parties with openly proto-nationalistic or nationalistic agendas. These included the reform-oriented Constitutional Party, which lobbied the French for municipal councils and more opportunities for Vietnamese to become French citizens, and the openly revolutionary Vietnam Nationalist Party (VNQDD) modeled on the Guomindang in China. The VNQDD's abortive uprising in 1930, crushed by the French, created an opening for yet another stream of Vietnamese nationalists, the Communists.

As a young man, Ho Chi Minh fled Vietnam when anti-French feelings were running high. In Britain and France and eventually in the new Soviet Union, he discovered socialism and then communism, whose unequivocal denunciation of colonialism he could heartily embrace. He became an early agent of the Comintern and in 1925 founded a revolutionary organization (Youth), the precursor of Vietnam's communist movement. Ho's subsequent maneuvering succeeded in uniting the colony's disparate Marxists and establishing a coherent party in 1930. His astute leadership combined with a talented group of adjutants—including Pham Van Dong and Vo Nguyen Giap—and France's suppression of their anti-Marxist nationalist rivals, account for the fact that, in Vietnam, Communists ultimately seized the leadership of the colony's national revolution.

Southeast Asia's first genuine nationalist revolution occurred in the Philippines in 1896, inspired by the reformist propagandizing of Jose Rizal and the revolutionary anger of Andres Bonifacio. In 1899, Filipino nationalists founded the first Republic of the Philippines, whose president, Emilio Aguinaldo, led the doomed effort at the turn of the twentieth century to fend off invading American armies. Once securely in power, the United States told its new Southeast Asian subjects that it was holding the colony in trusteeship; one day it would be theirs. It opened positions of senior leadership to elite Filipinos who soon became provincial governors and elected members of the colony-wide Philippine Assembly. By 1916 there was an elected senate as well. The colonial bureaucracy was also rapidly Filipinized.

In this way, elite Filipino families of the late Spanish era morphed into a new Americanizing elite under the United States. This situation muted revolutionary tendencies (some trade-union radicalism and a nascent communist movement notwithstanding) and created a class of wily collaborating nationalists who found their agency by clamoring for independence while at the same time reaping the benefits of public office. The Commonwealth of the Philippines, inaugurated in 1935 by the U.S. Congress, brought this process to a new stage. Manuel Quezon, archetypal politician of his day and leader of the Nacionalista Party, was elected president and led an entirely Filipino government under the watchful eyes of a U.S. high commissioner. As war clouds threatened in the late 1930s, Quezon hired U.S. general Douglas MacArthur to prepare for the defense of the colony. In the Philippines, nationalist hopes rested to the end with the Americans.

In the rest of Southeast Asia, nationalist sentiments were muted. Among the Malays in British territories, young men from princely families learned English and Western ways in school and came to see themselves as modern exemplars of their people; meanwhile, graduates of Malay vernacular-language schools harkened with some excitement to the nationalist movement in the nearby Dutch East Indies. But no one among either group emerged as dynamic nationalist leaders with politicized followings on a par with Sukarno, Aung San, Ho, or Quezon. The large Chinese populations of Malaya and the Straits Settlements were more politicized, but their concerns lay with the fate of China, not Southeast Asia. It was much the same elsewhere in Laos and Cambodia, where modern political stirrings were confined to a small group of French-educated elites and intellectuals whose concerns focused on Buddhism and on threats posed by Chinese and Vietnamese migrants. Tellingly, the party Ho Chi Minh founded in 1930 was the *Indochinese* Communist Party, but most of its members were Vietnamese.

And what about Siam, Southeast Asia's only sovereign state? Here the self-strengthening efforts of the Chakri kings Mongkut and Chulalongkorn succeeded in exposing a new generation of elite Thais to modern Western ideas. King Vajiravudh, Rama VI (r. 1910–1925), had been educated at Sandhurst and Oxford. Inspired by the heated nationalism of Europe, he propagated a jingoistic popular nationalism at home, complete with uniformed paramilitary scouts and anti-Chinese diatribes. Subsequently, as Siam's Westernized classes grew larger and more influential, their sense of being modern began to clash with the kingdom's absolute monarchy. Europe's monarchies were *constitutional* monarchies. In 1932, a conspiracy involving military and civilian activists orchestrated a bloodless coup d'état in which Siam's king Prajadhipok (Rama VII, r. 1925–1932) was subordinated to a constitution and parliament. The civilian and military governments that assumed power thereafter presided over an independent state that increasingly resembled the nations modeled on the West that other Southeast Asian nationalists were striving to achieve. In that spirit, in 1939, they adopted a conspicuously Western name for their country: Thailand.

A Japanese intervention

As the year 1940 approached, much of Southeast Asia was astir with nationalist hopes. In Burma, Indonesia, Vietnam, and the Philippines political movements with brilliant leaders were in play. And yet, aside from the Thais, already free, only Filipinos had any concrete hope for independence; the United States had promised it for 1946. Strive as they might, the others faced untold years of waiting and struggle.

Japan changed everything. Japan's modern march to empire had begun in the late nineteenth century as the Meiji government embarked on its quest to make Japan the equal of the world's great powers, namely, the Western empires. First in Taiwan (1895), then in Korea and Manchuria (1910 and 1931), and then in a large swath of the Chinese mainland (1937), the Japanese empire grew. As a rapidly industrializing and militarizing power, Japan drew essential raw materials from the colonies in Southeast Asia: copper, coal, iron ore, chromium, and petroleum.

In 1940, Japan's militarists established a beachhead in Indochina, where local French officials were collaborating with the Fascist-aligned Vichy government in France. After allying themselves with Germany and Italy in the Tripartite Pact of September 1940, they began planning to seize the rest of Southeast Asia.

In December 1941, Japan launched its attacks on two American colonies in the Pacific—Hawaii and the Philippines—as well as on British Malaya, British Burma, and Thailand. The Thais quickly capitulated and allied themselves with Japan. In Burma, young nationalists under Aung San and the Thakins led Japanese invaders into the British colony. In late 1941 and early 1942, forces of Imperial Japan swept triumphantly through British Malaya to Singapore and defeated the forces of the Netherlands in the Dutch East Indies. By April, General Douglas MacArthur and his Filipino-American forces in the Philippines had capitulated. For the first and only time in history, all Southeast Asia now fell under a single political domain. Japan called its new empire the Greater East Asia Co-Prosperity Sphere. It was to be *Asia for Asians*.

Some Southeast Asians welcomed the Japanese sincerely, others warily. Despite its appealing propaganda, Japan's urgent wartime priorities and military rule led to appalling brutalities. As British, Dutch, and Americans languished in improvised prison camps, ordinary Southeast Asians also suffered badly due to shortages of food, clothing, and common necessities such as soap. The Japanese forced some local women into sexual servitude and tens of thousands of Southeast Asian men into slave-like menial labor building roads, bridges, and railroads in distant sites.

The Japanese relied on Southeast Asian elites to continue functioning as officials. In places, they invited them to form whole governments. This occurred in Burma where Ba Maw became premier again under Japanese auspices, as his nationalist rival Aung San became minister of war and head of the new national army. In the Philippines, Jose Laurel, a Yale-educated member of the Philippine Supreme Court, headed another Japan-sponsored government as president. Both Ba Maw and Laurel met ceremoniously with Japan's war chief Hideki Tojo in Tokyo in 1943 on the occasion of the official "independence" of their occupied countries within the Co-Prosperity Sphere. Prince Wan Waithayakon of Thailand also attended the event in Tokyo. In Indonesia, Sukarno and a great many of his nationalist colleagues, including prominent Muslim leaders, lent their support to Japan's New Order in Asia as members of advisory bodies and propagandists for the empire in massive outdoor rallies.

In the occupied territories, collaboration with Japan was both an opportunity and a duty. If respected leaders did not come to the fore, local populations would be at the mercy of Japanese officers and unscrupulous opportunists. Remaining at the helm during wartime was also a way of sustaining one's place in society as larger power equations shifted unpredictably. A close relationship with Japanese officers could also provide useful leverage in strictly local power struggles.

But what if the Japanese were to lose the war? This became an issue after 1943 when news of the American advance across the Pacific began seeping into Southeast Asia. Some Southeast Asian collaborators appear to have placed all their hopes in Japan's promises. This was the case in Indonesia. But elsewhere, Southeast Asia's wartime leaders and elite actors responded strategically. In the Philippines, elite-connected anti-Japanese guerrillas were in contact with underground American agents throughout the war, alongside members of the Marxist-led Hukbalahap anti-Japanese peasant movement. Moreover, many in Manila's Japanese-sponsored government had close prewar ties to Americans and were well positioned to claim, later, that they accepted their wartime roles out of duty, not pro-Japanese sentiments. As for President Jose Laurel himself, one of his sons had been trained in the Japanese military academy and served with him in Manila during the war; another was serving with the Philippine government in exile in Washington.

In Burma, Aung San eventually used his wartime position as head of the Burmese national army to develop a clandestine anti-Japanese mass movement in collaboration with British and American agents. In Thailand, an underground Free Thai movement led by Pridi Banomyong, a prominent architect of Thailand's shift to constitutional monarchy and now regent to the underaged king, fostered ties with the British while the formal government kept up its public collaboration with Japan. As the winds of war blew evermore forcefully against Japan, these underground movements moved to the fore and assisted the Western Allied powers in their reconquest of the region.

In some parts of Southeast Asia, however, opposition to Japan was passionate from the outset. In Malaya, where the Malays and their sultans acquiesced to the occupation (with some supporting it enthusiastically), communist-leaning members of the local Chinese community formed the Malayan People's Anti-Japanese Army and struck out against the occupiers throughout the war in collaboration with British agents. And in Vietnam, Ho Chi Minh and his nascent communist movement mobilized a broad, popular armed movement to fight both the Japanese and the French. Under Ho's leadership, the Vietminh waxed strong amid wartime uncertainty and dearth, including a million-dead famine that struck Vietnam in 1945. That same year it collaborated with underground American agents in the final months of the war as it positioned itself for national leadership at war's end.

The Japanese occupation brought an end to the myth of white superiority. Not one Western power had withstood Japan, and Southeast Asians witnessed personally the humiliation of their former white bosses as they languished in wartime prison camps. In the meantime, many Southeast Asians welcomed the opportunity to rise to higher official positions by replacing now-absent whites and to undergo "can do" military training under the Japanese. Despite the deprivations of the war and the imminent return of Europeans, they faced the postwar years with heightened expectations. Nationalists stood poised to seize the moment.

Nations emerge

In some places, the region's colonizers acquiesced quickly. In the Philippines, the United States fulfilled its promise of independence on July 4, 1946. On that symbolic day, Manuel

Roxas, a member of the prewar elite of the American Philippines (and of the Japanese-sponsored wartime government) who had recently been elected president, stood before a crowd in Manila and declared that the Republic of the Philippines would henceforth "follow in the glistening wake of America's mighty prow." In Burma, Aung San's wartime mass movement, the Anti-Fascist People's Freedom League, emerged in the vanguard of independence efforts after the war. Aung San negotiated successfully with Britain and in 1947 was elected to lead the soon-to-be-independent government. His assassination by rivals that summer meant that someone else would claim this honor. On January 4, 1948, Aung San's longtime ally U Nu became premier of the Union of Burma.

Independence aspirations in Malaya were complicated by the absence of a passionate nationalist movement among Malays before the war and the presence of a communist-led, British-affiliated, Chinese independence movement during the war. Britain returned to Malaya with a blueprint for independence that aimed radically to alter the prewar status quo. Under the Malayan Union Plan, the old sultanates would be abandoned and all of Britain's subjects on the peninsula—Malay, Chinese, and Indian—would enjoy equal political rights in a unitary state. This plan acknowledged an important demographic truth, that by the late 1940s, Malaya's Chinese residents outnumbered (or at least equaled) the number of Malays.

Britain's plan for a Malayan Union catapulted the Malays into political action at last. Beginning in 1946, the colony's English-educated Malay elites mobilized around the United Malays National Organisation (UMNO) to rally Malays against the union plan and to lobby Britain for an alternative. They succeeded. A new plan in 1948 favored Malays in citizenship and official leadership and restored the nine historical states as well as their sultans, who would become constitutional monarchs in the planned parliamentary Federation of Malaya. The colony's communist-led Chinese activists immediately struck back in an armed rebellion that rattled the colony-in-transition for several years. Britain called it the Emergency and deployed its imperial armies to defeat the rebels with the support of UMNO and its Indian and Chinese partners—for many of Malaya's prosperous Chinese residents also opposed the radicals. Britain organized elections even as the fighting continued. The UMNO-led alliance prevailed, and on August 31, 1957, UMNO's Tunku Abdul Rahman, the newly elected premier, proclaimed freedom for the Federation of Malaya. In his speech he thanked Britain for "the assistance which we have received . . . along our long path to nationhood." Britain, Tunku said, "will ever find in us her best friend."

The French and the Dutch returned to Southeast Asia after the war as weakened states for whom empires still mattered dearly. Their postwar plans for Southeast Asia envisioned global federations of quasi-independent member states in which they would be the senior partners. This is not at all what Indonesian and Vietnamese nationalists had in mind.

In the final years of World War II, Sukarno and other leading Indonesian nationalists participated in Japan-fostered meetings to prepare for independence. A draft constitution was already in place on August 17, 1945, two days after Japan's surrender, when Sukarno seized the moment and declared Indonesia free. Soon afterward, partisans of the new Republic of Indonesia found themselves fending off returning Dutch troops, who occupied key urban areas as Sukarno and the Republic established free territories of their own. The often-violent standoff between the Republic and the Dutch—called the Indonesian Revolution— lasted four years and involved vexing negotiations interspersed with open warfare in which the Dutch army's superior weapons were poised against Indonesia's passionate cause and the home-ground advantage of its fighters. At first, the United States supported the Netherlands, but the exposure of Dutch atrocities and the Sukarno-led defeat of an internal Communist putsch

9. Sukarno was a Dutch-educated engineer who became Indonesia's first president. He believed that the force of nationalism itself could bring together the country's diverse peoples, religions, and ideologies.

gained favor for the Republic. In 1949, the Netherlands relinquished power to a federation of Indonesian states that gave way within a year to a unitary republic. Under the leadership of a relatively small group of Dutch-educated nationalists, the gargantuan tropical colony ruled for centuries by the Netherlands now became a nation.

In Vietnam the process of forming the nation was longer and bloodier. Like the Netherlands, France was loath to relinquish its colonies. Its postwar plan for a French Union ran headlong into the new Democratic Republic of Vietnam, whose independence Ho Chi Minh had proclaimed on September 2, 1945, quoting the American Declaration of Independence that "all men are created equal," with U.S. soldiers at the scene. By this time, Ho's organization, the Vietminh, controlled much of northern Vietnam and key areas of the center and south. France's return was enabled by its wartime ally, Britain, which occupied southern Vietnam as the Japanese departed. Instead of opting immediately for war, Ho agreed to place his government within France's French Union, but this arrangement broke down within a year.

The nine-year-long guerrilla war that followed was not precisely between the Vietnamese and the French. Despite the popular support and organizational acumen of the Vietminh—and the mantle of nationalism it bore—France had Vietnamese supporters as well. These included members of the colony's moneyed and propertied classes, its French-educated middle classes including military officers, and many Vietnamese Catholics and members of local religious sects. Significantly, Bao Dai, heir to the throne in Vietnam's Nguyen dynasty, agreed in 1949 to be head of state on the French side.

The Vietnamese on both sides of this conflict were nationalists, but they were nationalists with contrary hopes for the future of the nation. Communism divided them. This passionate disagreement drew the Vietnamese into the global crucible of the Cold War.

France's colonial armies and Vietnamese allies could not contain the surging Vietminh. By the early 1950s, the United States was subsidizing 80 percent of their flagging efforts as part of its postwar global mission to contain "the Reds" (as Ho and his followers now became in American propaganda). When Vietminh armies defeated France decisively in 1954 in the Battle of Dien Bien Phu, global Cold War factors more than local ones determined what happened next: the division of the country by the big powers (in the Geneva Accords) into Communist-led and non-Communist-led zones. Meant to be temporary, pending elections that were never held, these opposing zones hardened and prolonged Vietnam's decolonization for another twenty years.

In the north, the Democratic Republic under Ho Chi Minh and the Communist Party received support from the Soviet Union and China but claimed its legitimacy on the basis of its historical revolutionary achievement. It had many partisans south of the Geneva line, where the Republic of Vietnam, or South Vietnam, was blatantly beholden to its foreign sponsor, the United States. This significantly compromised its legitimacy. Even so, South Vietnam called upon the sincere loyalty of a great many Vietnamese for whom a Communist Vietnam was anathema and also upon the qualified and calculated support of many others for whom it was the better of two flawed options.

The hopeful project launched by the United States in South Vietnam unraveled quickly. The revolution soon reawakened in the south. Through the sustained, disciplined action of its highly committed partisans, the National Liberation Front (to Americans, the "Vietcong") ate deeply into the fragile body politic of the southern state. As the struggle intensified, the northern government and its guiding party engaged the fight in the south at ever-increasing levels, just as the United States escalated its military intervention in defense of its Cold War client. The carnage was stupendous for soldiers and civilians alike; between two and three million died. In the end, neither the efforts of the

South Vietnamese government nor the deployment at the war's peak of more than half a million U.S. soldiers nor the largest bombing campaign in history (against North Vietnam, Laos, and Cambodia) prevented the collapse of South Vietnam in April 1975.

The reunification of Vietnam that year marked the end of the country's decolonization. The dreams of nationhood planted long ago and proclaimed by Ho Chi Minh in 1945 had now come fully to fruition. The nation was claimed by its most successful nationalists, the Communists. Ho Chi Minh himself had died in 1969, but his party ruled on.

Inevitably, Vietnam's wrenching path to independence affected the fortunes of its Indochina neighbors, Laos and Cambodia. As its imperial fortunes waned in the early 1950s, France deftly relinquished its control in both would-be nations to their residual elites: in Cambodia to King Norodom Sihanouk, whose grand uncle (King Norodom) had invited the French into the kingdom ninety years before, and in Laos to a Royal Lao government led by Prince Souvanna Phouma, a neutralist, who together with his half-brother and ideological rival Prince Souphanouvong, dominated the small country's nascent political movements.

In the spirit of Cambodian nationhood, the French-educated Sihanouk abandoned the throne to become head of state and led his own political party as he fended off opponents from the left and the right. Brooking little opposition, he attempted to steer his country through the dangerous shoals of the Cold War through the 1950s and 1960s. Clashing bitterly with the United States, he refused to take sides in the war exploding next door in Vietnam, which inevitably bled across his borders; the Communist command center for the war in South Vietnam (COSVN) lay *just* within Cambodia, for example. The United States maneuvered for regime change and, in 1970, Sihanouk was overthrown by one of his generals; Lon Nol immediately led Cambodia into war on the U.S. and South Vietnamese side. Intensive U.S. bombing inside the country now accompanied chaotic ground fighting. All this led to a bitter end in 1975 with the capture of the state by the surging Khmer Rouge.

In Laos, the war in Vietnam penetrated early and deeply. The northeast plateau became an important part of the clandestine corridor through which the North Vietnamese fostered the revolution in the south. In collaboration, Prince Souphanouvong led the Pathet Lao, or Lao Communists. To push back, the United States recruited Laotian hill peoples, such as the Hmong, into clandestine anti-communist armies that fought a "secret war" alongside American agents throughout the long struggle. Meanwhile, in Vientiane, neutralist and pro-U.S. regimes (with Souvanna Phouma as the key player) by turns attempted to hold the center together. Amid this chaotic web of power struggles the Pathet Lao advanced. And it was they who assumed power at war's end in 1975. All former French Indochina was now reconfigured into Marxist-led nations of one sort or another.

By this time, the fledgling Federation of Malaya had expanded to incorporate two remaining pieces of Britain's erstwhile Southeast Asian empire: Sarawak, once the British-protected private domain of the Brooke family, and Sabah, formerly the private commercial domain of the British North Borneo Company. In 1963 these Borneo territories were folded into a new national entity named Malaysia, along with Singapore, the richest and most populous of Britain's Chinese-populated Straits Settlements. Singapore's highly politicized population was led by Lee Kuan Yew, the dynamic Cambridge-educated trade-union lawyer and head of the colony's left-leaning People's Action Party (PAP). Lee and his aroused Chinese constituents were not a good fit in the expanded Malay-led federation of Malaysia. In 1965, Singapore withdrew and, with Lee and his party at the helm, embarked upon its own future as an independent nation.

A few years later, in 1984, the Sultanate of Brunei relinquished its protected status under Britain and became, once again, a sovereign kingdom under its Sandhurst-educated sultan, an absolute monarch.

The nature of nations

As in the kingdoms of the past, in Southeast Asia's nations indigenous leaders once again took their places at the top of the social and political pyramid. New men and women of prowess rose to become elected politicians, political party bosses, power-seizing generals, and dictators, as well as leaders in fields encompassing education, health, law, journalism, and business. The anomaly of foreign rule was past. But the legacy of foreign rule was deep. In many respects, the new nations resembled the former Western colonies much more than they resembled the region's bygone kingdoms.

To begin with, both the spatial and the conceptual configurations of Southeast Asia's nations followed that of the colonies. The nations were geo-bodies, whose territories were mapped and whose official authority extended fully to the borders instead of attenuating away from the capital, mandala-style. For the most part, the maps of the colonies prefigured the maps of the nations, so that outlying rings of the old mandalas that had been captured and colonized by Western powers became part of the new nations—just as nationalists had envisioned.

In the islands, the impact of colonial conquest and mapping was radical. Unlike the mainland where modern nations overlay historic mandalas in Burma, Thailand, and Cambodia, in the islands the new nations represented wholly novel configurations created by Western empires. Although modern Indonesians like to think of their country as a modern incarnation of the great mandala kingdom of Majapahit, nothing remotely like the Dutch East Indies existed in Southeast Asia before the Dutch created it. Yet it was this exact colonial geo-body that Indonesian nationalists dreamed of as their own nation. The modern Philippines is another obvious example. As a geo-body, Las Philipinas was a Spanish creation.

Malaysia is an extreme case. Britain became the hegemon in Malaya partly as a result of its treaty with the Netherlands in 1824 identifying the Melaka Straits as the borderline between English and Dutch spheres of influence. Malaya became "British" and subsequently Malaysian. Sumatra, the home of a great number of Malays, became "Dutch" and therefore Indonesian. That the north coast of Borneo would be colonized by Britain-affiliated privateers was largely serendipitous. But when Sarawak and North Borneo (Sabah) were orphaned by their private owners following World War II, Britain took them over and, seventeen years later, arranged for them to join Malaysia, a wholly accidental configuration that is unquestionably a nation today.

Finally, tiny East Timor underscores the point. Its half of the remote island of Timor (plus another small enclave) was a Portuguese presence that the Dutch let stand even as the Dutch East Indies grew all around it. It remained separate when the Indies became Indonesia and remains so today, despite a brutal twenty-four-year-long attempt by the dictator Suharto to make it part of Indonesia after Portugal withdrew in 1975. East Timor proved indigestible and became its own sovereign nation in 2002. Its nationalist leaders named Portuguese as the national language. Even in this small place, empire was destiny.

Colonialism shaped the new nations in other ways as well. Southeast Asia's nationalists longed for independence but embraced Western political ideas and other lessons of their colonizers. They created governments that built upon British, French, Dutch, and American models for their bureaucracies and for ministries of education, public works, finance, and foreign affairs. They created parliamentary democracies, presidential democracies, and Leninist one-party states. They established militaries with service branches, titles, and uniforms similar to those of the West.

They wrote constitutions. And they created educational systems based on textbooks, schoolrooms, and curriculums mirroring those of Western schools, including instruction in Western languages. All of these things enabled them to place their new states within the global matrix of modern nations.

Other legacies of colonialism were more problematic. Beyond a thin layer of Western-educated elites, most of Southeast Asia's new nations possessed large populations of poorly educated, semiliterate citizens. (In 1950, only Thailand and the Philippines possessed literacy rates above 50 percent.) Few were prepared to staff their ballooning bureaucracies with qualified personnel or their schools with qualified teachers. Moreover, the economies of Southeast Asia were overwhelmingly agricultural and industrially primitive. A total of 50 to 70 percent or more of the region's population was rural. The Western regimes had introduced little in the way of manufacturing and processing. Southeast Asia exported rubber, tin, coffee, tea, sugar, and the like and imported practically all its manufactured consumer goods and machinery, including cars, trucks, pumps, and printing presses.

The new nations of Southeast Asia had inadequate electric power, a poor network of roads and railroads, and few hospitals and doctors. In 1960, Indonesia counted one doctor for every 70,000 people. Poverty was widespread and in many places the norm. On average, the GDP per capita in Southeast Asia in the early postwar years was well under U.S.$300 dollars a year. In the eyes of the West, Southeast Asia was backward. It was the Third World.

Yet another legacy of colonialism weighed heavily. The fact that colonial maps became national maps meant that most of the new nations included within their boundaries territories occupied by ethnic groups that, historically, had been rivals or enemies of the nation's ruling group. These animosities flared anew after independence in Burma, Indonesia, the Philippines, and elsewhere.

The Cold War and authoritarianism

Many of these issues were complicated by ideology. The Cold War placed Southeast Asians, inadvertently, within one of the world's great contested arenas. China's revolutionary embrace of communism, the subsequent war in Korea, and the leading role of Ho Chi Minh in Vietnam's national revolution raised fears in the West and especially in the United States that all Southeast Asia would potentially "fall." This is what lay behind the long, losing campaign of the United States in Vietnam and in nearby Laos and Cambodia.

Elsewhere things played out differently. In the Philippines, a communist-led anti-Japanese movement known as the Hukbalahap grew strong during the Japanese occupation and mobilized peasants around a land-to-the-tiller program. After independence, the new nation's elite politicians criminalized the Huks and blocked their elected representatives from the legislature. In the subsequent campaign to defeat their armed movement, the United States found a compelling political ally in Ramon Magsaysay. As national defense chief and subsequently president, Magsaysay orchestrated aggressive anti-insurgency strategies alongside sociopolitical measures to address Huk grievances (including opening homesteading land to poor farmers). Magsaysay was unabashedly pro-American and told Filipino voters that their vulnerable nation was safer with the United States as a friend.

The post–World War II leaders of Thailand agreed. Under Field Marshal Sarit Thanarat and the generals Thanom Kittikachorn and Praphat Charusathien, Thailand fell into step with American Cold War policy, joining the Southeast Asia Treaty Organization (SEATO) in 1954 and steadfastly supporting American policy in Indochina while fiercely suppressing its own communist and left-wing students and activists. In Malaya, the Communist-led insurgency was also defeated. In each of these cases, substantial amounts of Cold War foreign aid flowed to the collaborating regimes. By the mid-1960s, Thailand, Malaysia, Singapore, and the Philippines were firmly in the anticommunist group as the fates of Vietnam, Laos, and Cambodia were still being contested.

Sihanouk's strategy of remaining free of Cold War conflicts by declaring neutrality in Cambodia found adherents in Burma and Indonesia. General Ne Win, who seized power in Burma in 1962, and Sukarno, Indonesia's founding president, both favored nonalignment. Indeed, Sukarno hosted the first world summit of nonaligned countries in Indonesia in 1955. At Bandung, he spoke for the "voiceless ones in the world" who were now coming into their own.

Unlike Ne Win, who led his country into isolation, Sukarno accepted aid from both sides, exasperating both in the process. As president, he presided over a striking array of political parties, from conservative Muslims on the one side to Communists on the other. His embrace of the surging Communists as political allies in the late 1950s and early 1960s, along with his anti-imperialist, anti-American rhetoric, won him the animosity of the United States. Washington supported a rebellion against him in 1958 and subsequently conspired with members of his officer corps to eliminate the Indonesian Communists. The Communist Party was legal in Indonesia and by 1963 claimed as many as two million members and ten million affiliates. Its annihilation in the army-led massacres of 1965–1966 removed communism as a political factor in Indonesia, ended Sukarno's career, and brought a pro-United States military dictatorship to power under Suharto. He ruled for thirty-three years.

Indonesia's turn to dictatorship exemplified a trend. By this time the early postindependence experiments in parliamentary democracy had also failed in Burma, where General Ne Win would rule even longer than Suharto. Generals ruled in Thailand, too. The Philippines soon shifted in an authoritarian direction as well when, in 1972, the two-term elected president Ferdinand Marcos declared martial law—to contain a communist threat, he said. Marcos ruled with American support until 1986.

The turn to authoritarian government in Southeast Asia, including the triumph of one-party rule in the Indochina states and in Singapore under Lee Kuan Yew, is perhaps a reflection of the enormous task of transforming colonies into nations. Many of the region's formative nationalists entertained visions of national societies in which citizens governed themselves through a process of democratic consensus. This proved romantic. They had not accounted for the power of lingering ethnic and regional animosities, for the corrosive impact of poverty, for the explosive appeal of utopian ideologies and their disciplined movements, nor for the machinations of great outside powers. Nor had they accounted for the visceral appeal of power itself as they and their elite peers competed with each other in the uncharted seas of nationhood.

The neighborhood matures

Many Southeast Asians alive in the late 1970s had lived through the entire transformation of their societies from colonies to nations. Surveying the region, they might have despaired. By 1975, the dust had settled in Vietnam but the trauma had yet to end as refugees by the tens of thousands fled the newly reunited country for years to come. Neighboring Cambodia was lost to atrocity behind the bloody veil of the Khmer Rouge, who murdered or otherwise caused to die about one-third of the country's population. A thousand miles away in East Timor, the inhabitants were reeling in resistance to an armed invasion by Indonesia. Burma languished under a military dictator, Ne Win, and the Philippines under a civilian one, Marcos. Suharto and the army dominated Indonesia. And in Thailand, a student-led movement for democracy in the mid-1970s brought about three years of civilian government only to be brutally overtaken by military rule once again. Moreover, with the exception of Singapore, Southeast Asia remained an archetypal Third World region, still poor and still in the throes of its own halting creation.

Yet at this very time, Southeast Asia stood on the verge of region-changing events. In 1976, ASEAN's members signed the groundbreaking Treaty of Amity and Cooperation in Southeast Asia, paving the way for region-wide cooperation. In late 1978, Vietnam launched its ten-year occupation of Cambodia that brought an end to the Killing Fields and inaugurated Cambodia's return to coherency. Only a few years later, Vietnam inaugurated the *doi moi* reforms that opened its economy to market forces and rapid growth. Almost simultaneously, the People Power Revolution of 1986 led by Corazon Aquino overthrew the Marcos dictatorship in the Philippines and restored the country's vibrant oligarchic democracy. Two years later, in 1988, a democracy movement in Burma led by Aung San's daughter, Aung San Suu Kyi, openly defied Burma's military junta and set into motion a series of events leading to consequential reforms in coming decades.

Next, the collapse of the Soviet Union in 1991 brought the Cold War and its distorting impact to an end. This major event made it possible for Southeast Asia's nations led by Communist and non-Communist parties to focus more on their similarities than on their differences. By 1999, Vietnam, Laos, Cambodia, and Burma had all joined the neighborhood association, ASEAN. Meanwhile, beginning in 1978, the ascendance of Deng Xiaoping in China set off a series of reforms that would soon transform China and have colossal repercussions for Southeast Asia.

Southeast Asia soon experienced its first postindependence boom. Beginning around 1990, new investment from Japan, North America, and Europe began lifting the regional economies, especially those of Malaysia, Thailand, Indonesia, and the Philippines, where economies began expanding at rates between 5 and 10 percent a year. Export processing zones and investor-friendly laws brought high-tech manufacturing into the region alongside a rise in low-tech, low-wage manufacturing. Cities blossomed with new construction as L-shaped cantilever cranes dominated the rising skylines of Bangkok, Jakarta, and Manila. Property values rose. So did incomes and opportunities for the rising number of the region's high school and university graduates. Middle classes expanded. Upper classes luxuriated— new golf courses sprouted everywhere. The region took on a new glow. People spoke of Southeast Asia's New Tigers, meaning Singapore, Malaysia, and Thailand. The Philippines called itself a "cub."

This exuberant period came crashing to an end in 1997. Beginning in Thailand, a monetary crisis swept the region. The decline of Japan's yen alongside Southeast Asia's poorly regulated banks, risky loans, and endemic corruption all fostered the crash. Southeast Asia was soon littered with bankruptcies and empty high-rise apartments. Abandoned half-built hotels and office buildings stood exposed like skeletons as legions of hopeful young MBAs, engineers, and professionals lost their jobs.

The impact of the crash was not permanent but it had consequences. In Indonesia it contributed to the fall of President Suharto, for example, who resigned in the face of popular protests in 1998. This surprising event led to a dynamic new period of democratization in Indonesia, known as *reformasi*. (The country's latest two presidents, Bambang Susilo Yudhoyono and Joko Widodo were both popularly elected.) The end of military dictatorship in Indonesia also paved the way for East Timor's independence. In a 1999 popular referendum authorized by Suharto's successor, the people of East Timor voted overwhelmingly in favor of separation from Indonesia. Indonesia's withdrawal was vengeful and bloody, but in 2002 East Timor became a fully sovereign nation, Southeast Asia's eleventh.

After 1997, the region slowly recovered, faltered again in the early 2000s, and recovered again in a pattern that continues. Each small boom intensifies the region's links to the larger world economy and brings new levels of economic diversity and sophistication to its manufacturing and financial sectors, as well as to its huge and still expanding agribusiness and mining sectors. This growth is asymmetrical. Southeast Asia has both very rich and very poor countries. In all but Malaysia, Singapore, Thailand, and Brunei, the very poor (people earning less than U.S.$3.10 a day) still account for more than 30 percent of the national populations.

Even so, Southeast Asia today is a far cry from Southeast Asia of early independence. Over the decades, a stable region has taken shape. The new states are intact. And, along with the rest of Asia—including India, Japan, South Korea, Taiwan, and China—they are wholly engaged with and embraced within today's global matrix of nation-states and the world capitalist economy.

Chapter 5
The past is in the present

Today's fast-changing Southeast Asians seem utterly engaged with the present. Among them, 45 percent are under fifteen years of age. Like young people everywhere, they participate in a mixing of popular culture that fuses global elements with local ones; social media links them to each other and to the world as never before. The lucky and ambitious ones are definitely learning English.

Meanwhile, the great stone monuments and temple complexes that marked the centers of old mandala kingdoms are tourist attractions today. So are the once-grand colonial hotels that were havens of luxury for world-traveling Westerners during the high age of colonies; think of the Raffles in Singapore, the Strand in Yangon (the former Rangoon). Many of the imperial government buildings and gracious ruling-class homes of the colonial era have been repurposed as museums, shops, and restaurants or remodeled as residences for today's elites. Dense populations and traffic jams are a given. Even in provincial cities and towns, motorbikes and noisy motorized tricycles and minicabs clutter the streets, jostling with a growing number of automobiles. Nationalities are taken for granted. One is Singaporean, Malaysian, Filipino, Thai. These identities feel permanent, eternal. ASEAN gatherings featuring ritual photographs of Southeast Asian heads of state standing side by side emblemize the coherence of the ten-nation neighborhood. Other facts of life include the cities' dirty air and filthy water and shorelines and beaches awash with the world's trash. Such is Southeast Asia of the moment.

What remains today of the past? Of Southeast Asia's kingdoms and colonies and its first-draft nations? Despite the distractions of the busy present, the answer is quite a lot.

The extraordinary heterogeneity of Southeast Asia has not changed. Beneath the skin of the region's national identities— Filipinos, Indonesians, Singaporeans, and so on—thousands of separate ethnicities and languages and dialects remain, playing a role in local power struggles and sometimes in national ones. In places, ethnic competitions have led to violence, especially where migrating outsiders compete with long-established residents and where ethnic differences are compounded by religious ones. This has occurred in eastern Indonesia, for example, where in-migrant Javanese Muslims have clashed with Christian Malukans and Papuans. The Muslim Rohingya are a despised minority among

10. Southeast Asian leaders meet at the 2016 ASEAN-UN Summit. The ten members of ASEAN have pledged to respect each other's sovereignty and to renounce the use of force in their relations with each other.

Buddhist Burmans. And so on. Everywhere, power-wielding majorities lord it over regional minorities in a hierarchy of size and influence. These big-fish–small-fish rivalries are much discussed and figure in countless stereotypes and jokes—as when Filipino Tagalogs speak about Cebuanos, or the other way around. In multiethnic Indonesia, the possibilities are legion.

Hill peoples are still thought of as backward by ethnic-majority lowlanders and are subjected to predatory policies by national governments that have opened their ancestral lands to logging, mining, and agribusiness. These days the hills are no longer apart. Southeast Asia's swidden farmers have been pinched into ever smaller pockets of the decreasing forests, just as wildlife has been. Hill farmers and their children have become wageworkers. Many now live in logging camps and mining towns and in the burgeoning provincial cities that flourish as exchange centers for logs, palm oil, coffee, copper, and a slew of other commodities. When they don their traditional finery of brightly dyed textiles, beads, feathers, and metalwork, it is likely to be for a special ritual or festival, or for world-traveling backpackers. In places where these changes have not yet occurred, as in upland Laos, national governments are committed to bringing them about quickly.

The plains are also changing. In the region's vast, flat lowlands, rice paddies still stretch into the distance. Rice is still the staple food for most Southeast Asians. But the economic disadvantages of farming and the region's prospering cities and towns continue to draw people from farms into the expanding urban economy, including the gray economy of city slums. (By 2010, some 42 percent of Southeast Asians had become urbanites.) The urban invasion of rice-paddy land is striking. On the outskirts of Southeast Asian cities, now replete with housing subdivisions, industrial parks, and pop-up commercial centers with fast food and petrol stations, one sees everywhere the earthen remains of former paddy-field bunds.

Power is money

Southeast Asians were early participants in commerce. The region's men of prowess—its kings, rajas, and sultans—amassed power by controlling large numbers of people who channeled resources toward their capitals. Throughout the mainland and the islands, they built and enriched their mandala centers by managing, taxing, and participating in trade.

Colonialism interrupted this pattern as Western colonial regimes and capitalists seized these opportunities for themselves. This was blatantly obvious in the behavior of the East India companies, but the crusading Iberians also created fortified trade hubs in Melaka and Manila for the same purposes. Later, more mature colonial states left commerce to private companies—think Michelin, British Petroleum, American Tobacco—and raised revenues from the taxes, levies, and fines they imposed upon their subjects.

The colonial apparatuses for managing and taxing trade and for revenue collection were inherited by the leaders of Southeast Asia's nations at independence. They enabled the region's new leaders to begin recapturing the profits of regional trade and local natural resources for the nation itself, and also for themselves. Southeast Asia's new men of prowess—elected politicians, dictators and strongmen, party leaders, and generals in power—imposed new tariffs and joint-venture laws, licensing requirements, and facilities fees; they cut profit-sharing deals with major agribusiness and mining companies; and, in some cases, they expropriated foreign-owned companies and strategic sectors of the economy altogether. Indonesia's Sukarno nationalized petroleum, for example.

In a similar way, new laws strove to marginalize Chinese participation in national economies and to redistribute Chinese wealth. Conspicuous examples of this include Indonesia and the

Philippines, where ethnic Chinese merchants were driven from their rural shops in the 1950s, and Malaysia, where the New Economic Policy beginning in 1971 sought to move more of the nation's potential wealth into Malay hands. Southeast Asia's ruling elites also used their influence to garner private fees, gifts, and bribes for opening doors to some business suitors and closing them to others. In many formal and informal ways, they have enriched themselves and their cronies and followers (including their citizens) in a pattern reminiscent of rulers in the age of kingdoms. Then as now, in Southeast Asia, power is money.

The lion's share of goods that enter and leave Southeast Asia, from tea, coffee, and sugar to petroleum, copper ore, coal, and every sort of consumer good, still goes by ship. As in the past, the harbor towns of Southeast Asia do a brisk business. To get a modern sense of the historic importance of classic maritime entrepôts such as Melaka, one can do no better than visit today's Singapore, the second busiest seaport in the world. Here immense container docks go on and on for miles on the island's south shore.

Singapore, famously free of the every-hand-is-out sort of corruption that plagues other countries in the region, illustrates the connection between political power and wealth accumulation. In this prosperous one-party state led by the People's Action Party (PAP), average citizens have done very well. Singapore is a First World country with a higher per capita gross domestic product (GDP) than the United States. The island nation's political elites have also done very well. Singapore's non-bribe-taking senior ministers and bureaucrats are paid salaries that surpass those of their regional peers by many multiples. Lee Hsien Loong, the current prime minister and son of founder Lee Kuan Yew, is the highest paid head of state in the world. Members of elite ruling-party families including the Lees have placed themselves comfortably among the island's business, financial, and professional top tier. In Singapore, everything is strictly legal. (Still, power is money.)

Sleeping mandalas

Southeast Asia's Western colonies and its new nation-states imposed upon the region a well-delineated matrix of states with clear borders; they are geo-bodies. What remains, then, of the mandalas of old? The impressive survival of the new states since independence and their formal incorporation into a web of international organizations, including ASEAN, suggest that Southeast Asia's nations are here to stay. Nation-building has succeeded in Southeast Asia. Nationalism is a force. And yet, Southeast Asia remains rife with conflict. Borders are porous. Certain regions remain astir. Others lie uneasily within the nation. Often, sleeping mandalas provide an explanation.

Thailand illustrates this point. Under the Chakri kings of the nineteenth century, Siam's mandala stretched deeply into the Malay Peninsula and embraced a wide swath of territory in western Cambodia. In typical mandala fashion, this huge domain had grown at the expense of others.

To the south, the Thais had subjugated several small Malay Muslim kingdoms that had once been part of the great mandala centered at Melaka. These included Patani, Kedah, Perlis, Trengganu, and Kelantan and their Malay-Muslim subjects. By the mid-nineteenth century, these mini-states were all under Thai sway. In 1909, however, the king of Siam, Chulalongkorn, ceded four of them to Britain, and they became part of British Malaya. Patani remained part of the Thai state; its Malay-Muslim subjects therefore remained on the Thai side of the border.

To the east, the immense mandala of Angkor had once included much of eastern Thailand. In the nineteenth century, the Chakri kings were reversing this process, aggressively attaching Battambang and Siem Reap and neighboring Khmer territories to the Thai mandala. This was one reason that King Norodom of Cambodia accepted French protection in 1863; in 1904, the French wrested the territories back when King Chulalongkorn ceded them to French Cambodia.

During World War II, Japan rewarded its Thai allies by allotting the Malay and Cambodian territories to Thailand, but they were restored to the British and French at war's end. This arrangement became fixed in the region's new nations. Today, Patani and other Malay-Muslim territories lie in Thailand, while Kedah, Trengganu, Perlis, and Kelantan are part of Malaysia. Meanwhile, Battambang and Siem Reap lie within Cambodia's geo-body. In short, the national borders of today's Malaysia, Thailand, and Cambodia lie athwart ancient mandala cusps that have been fluid as recently as seventy years ago.

Flash forward. Today, about 1.5 million Malay-speaking Muslims live in Thailand's "Muslim south," an area long awash in conflict and violence between its Malay-descended residents and the Thai authorities. These conflicts are usually described in religious terms—Muslim rebels, extremists, and separatists act out against the Buddhist Thai state. But the deeper roots of conflict lie in colonial-era border fixing and subsequent nation-building, which have interrupted the more fluid mandala patterns of classical Southeast Asia and rendered the Malays of southern Thailand a restless Muslim minority within a modern Buddhist nation.

Tensions of a different kind have arisen on the border between Thailand and Cambodia. Following the back-and-forth territorial shifts during World War II, this area remained problematic during the turbulent years of the Khmer Rouge and its aftermath in Cambodia. Beginning in the 1970s, refugee camps sprang up all along the long, mountainous Thai-Cambodian border as wave after wave of people fled the unfolding violence and atrocities. In a rugged garland of disparate refugee camps, tens of thousands of displaced people lived in limbo awaiting new homes abroad or an opening to return to Cambodia. The formal jurisdiction of both the Thais and Cambodians was highly compromised in this violent and fluid frontier along an age-old Southeast Asian mandala cusp.

Tensions flowed along this same border in 2008 over the ownership of Preah Vihear Temple. This one-thousand-year-old temple was one of thousands of Hindu/Buddhist cult temples that the Khmers of Angkor built throughout their giant mandala that penetrated deep into today's Thailand. This one lies along the current border. According to old French maps and a 1962 judgment by the International Court of Justice, Preah Vihear Temple lies in Cambodia.

In 2008, however, Cambodia's application to UNESCO to designate Preah Vihear a World Heritage Site aroused Thai politicians to claim the temple site for Thailand. Tempers flared, and in the next few years fighting broke out sporadically between Thai and Cambodian soldiers along the border. Passionate nationalist feelings stirred around the conflict, which was finally resolved in 2013 when the International Court of Justice declared the area a demilitarized zone. Why did this small temple and its ambient site matter so much? For both sides, the conflict recalls mandala contests that go back many centuries. This is remembered, even though, these days, the fight is cast in terms of national sovereignty. Like the conflict in southern Thailand, this one still simmers. More than a dozen similarly contested areas exist along the same long border.

We can identify another sleeping mandala in the Sulu Zone of maritime Southeast Asia. In the age of kingdoms, the Sulu Sea was a great field of mandala contestation, with small sultans and rajas and local big men dominating its island and riverine states. Spain took much of this territory out of competition by the 1600s, leaving Mindanao and its neighboring polities in play. This vast maritime theater of trading and raiding was famous for pearls, tortoise shells, and sea delicacies, and it was also the center of

Southeast Asia's maritime slave market with its center at Jolo. It was here that the sultan of Sulu held sway. He claimed a mandala that included most of the islands and small polities of the zone and that stretched to the northeast coast of Borneo. This area was also claimed by a competing sultan whose capital was in Brunei. Northeast Borneo thus lay on a mandala cusp, with one mandala pulling it toward Jolo, the other toward Brunei.

When the North Borneo Company acquired northeast Borneo in 1881 as the site for its agribusiness enterprises, it signed arrangements with both sultans. North Borneo came under British protection and was later absorbed directly into the British Empire. As a result, it subsequently became Sabah, a constituent state of modern Malaysia. Meanwhile, American colonizers in the Philippines brought the sultan of Sulu to heel, and his subordinate territories eventually became part of today's Republic of the Philippines.

This mandala-world and colonial-era backstory explains the repeated attempts by Filipino politicians to "reclaim" Sabah. The sultan of Sulu, they say, only *leased* North Borneo to the North Borneo Company; he did not sell it. Such efforts stir nationalist feelings but inevitably fail. In today's world the national geo-bodies are stronger than the underlying mandalas. Still, the Sulu Zone remains an arena where goods and people flow freely across soft borders. And Sabah is still on the cusp—close to a million Filipinos now live there.

The mandala dynamics of the Sulu Zone also help to explain the unrelenting violence and political conflict of the southern Philippines. Recall that this area was already Muslim when Spain arrived in the 1500s and that Spain never wholly controlled it. Instead, a variety of ethnic groups, including the seafaring Badjau, Tausug, and Sama Dilaut, competed for followers and resources among themselves, and, at times, they deferred to regional mandala centers. Large and small, they were led by proud sultans and warrior chiefs and clans claiming royal status.

American armies quelled these independent societies in the late 1800s, and they became part of the American Philippines. When the Republic of the Philippines became independent in 1946, these Muslim territories were involuntarily folded into the Christian nation. Most of the conflicts of the past seventy years, including wars of succession, movements for autonomy, and the penetration of the region by radical Islamists, can be traced to this event and to its postindependence consequences. These include the migration of Christian Filipinos into once majority-Muslim areas and the repeated and sometimes violent attempts by the Philippine government to integrate its Muslim South into the geo-body of the nation.

Another arena of contemporary unrest in Southeast Asia that can be understood in part through mandala dynamics is the catastrophe of the Rohingya in Myanmar. Their homeland in Arakan lies over an old mandala cusp dividing Muslim Bengal and Buddhist Burma. Britain's colonization of both areas led Arakan into the geo-body of British Burma and, hence, subsequently in 1948, into the independent Union of Burma, today's Myanmar.

As a consequence, the Muslim Arakanese, or Rohingya, became unwanted subjects within a nation that defined itself as Buddhist. This led to years of harassment by the group's Buddhist neighbors in Rakhine State (as Arakan is known today) and repression by the Burmese government itself: in 1982 dictator Ne Win denied them citizenship as Bengali "foreigners." (Currently this applies to more than eight hundred thousand people.) Buddhist-Muslim hostilities, rebellion, and reprisals ensued, all leading to the crisis of 2015 and after, in which tens of thousands of desperate, stateless Rohingya refugees have fled Myanmar for uncertain futures in Bangladesh, Malaysia, Indonesia, and Thailand.

Like the Rohingya, the Shans, Karen, and Kachin of Myanmar are also restless within the nation. Their territories, once small mandala polities in their own right, were also included within the huge mandala of the Konbaung kings that Britain seized in the nineteenth century. They, too, became part of British Burma and were subsequently included in the official geo-body of the Union of Burma at independence in 1948. Almost immediately, rebellions erupted in these outlying non-Burman territories, challenging the new nation's fragile parliamentary government and leading to, among other things, the triumph of the army as the dominant institution in Burma.

Throughout the ensuing decades, entities such as the Shan State Army, the Chin National Front, the Kachin Independence Army, the Karen National Union, the United Wa State Army, and others governed their territories in defiance of the Union of Burma, sometimes funding their armies and shadow states with profits from opium grown in the Golden Triangle. War between the armies of the center and the armies of the periphery dragged on and on, leaving a record of appalling brutality in its wake, plus waves of refugees who made their way into neighboring Thailand. Myanmar's current membership in ASEAN may serve to reinforce the nation's territorial claims, and new governments since 2011 have been negotiating an end to the long wars with more than a dozen armed groups. (Eight such groups signed a cease-fire agreement in 2015). Yet as Myanmar moves gingerly away from military rule, it remains to be seen whether the nation will succeed in its efforts to unify.

Myanmar's fragility is exceptional. Even as sleeping mandalas stir beneath today's geo-bodies and underlie certain contemporary disturbances, Southeast Asia's nations show every sign of enduring.

India and China

Thinking of the deep structures of Southeast Asia's formation, what can we observe about India and China, the two radiating civilizations from which Southeast Asians borrowed so much?

Of these two, India was formative, shaping the major societies of most of the mainland and islands over centuries as Hindu- and Buddhist-inflected civilizations and contributing to the Islamization of the islands as well. A great deal of India's influence remains in layer upon layer of language, culture, and custom throughout the region. Millions of Southeast Asians bear names from the classical Indian story cycles; in Indonesia, many a young couple gets married in regalia that harken back to the epics. Buddhism and Islam are the hegemonic religious cultures; in Bali, a brilliant Southeast Asian Hinduism survives.

But it is hard to find examples of contemporary borrowing from India, aside from the popularity of Bollywood films. Southeast Asians are not learning Indian languages—unless you mean English—although they will still sometimes reach into Sanskrit to find an appropriate-sounding name for something modern (as an alternative to using an English word). Trade between India and Southeast Asia pales in comparison to the region's trade with others. The South Asian community in Southeast Asia tends to be small and concentrated in Malaysia and Singapore, with expatriates scattered about elsewhere. As India rises to prosperity and influence, this will surely change. But as of now, it is Asia's other great radiating civilization that looms large in Southeast Asia's present: China.

The impact of China's long ties and waves of migration to Southeast Asia is permanent. Today, the Southeast Asian Chinese control a large swath of the regional economy, despite the ever larger participation of indigenous Southeast Asians. Overcoming stigmatizing stereotypes and a variety of laws and policies designed to curb their influence in the region's independent nations, they have continued to thrive. One key to their success is a region-wide network of families and interconnected businesses that transcends the national economies. Links of kinship, dialect, and mutual trust foster business ties and expedite transactions across a vast "offshore" Chinese matrix that has flourished even in times when China itself has languished.

After its reunification under Mao Zedong and the Communist Party, China began wielding influence in Southeast Asia by supporting Ho Chi Minh's revolution in Vietnam and, to a lesser degree, fostering other communist movements in the region. In 1955, Chou Enlai made a point of attending Sukarno's nonaligned summit at Bandung.

Yet the People's Republic of China remained largely preoccupied with itself until after the Cultural Revolution and Mao's death in 1976. As China subsequently began to ratchet up its market economy under Deng Xiaoping, the offshore Chinese community in Southeast Asia came rapidly into play. Money being held in Bangkok, Jakarta, Singapore, Manila, and Kuala Lumpur could now be invested profitably in China. And money being generated in China could be invested in Southeast Asia.

In the 1990s, capital flows between Southeast Asia and China began to rise. In the next decade they soared. The existence of a region-wide matrix of Chinese families and businesses made this possible. For the first time in centuries, the economy of China became a driving variable in the economy of Southeast Asia. Today Chinese money and goods are pouring into the region. Like the Walmarts of the United States, the shopping centers and markets of Southeast Asia are chock-full of Chinese-made consumer goods, from nuts and bolts and pins to light bulbs, electric fans, air conditioners, television sets, and motorcycles. These products are imported by long-established Chinese-owned companies already on the spot. At the same time, investments from China are funding hydroelectric dams, hotels and casinos, agribusiness plantations, factories, and mines, and ambitious railway projects connecting Southeast Asian cities to Chinese cities.

A very large shift is underway. After two centuries of decline and turmoil, China is re-staking its historical claim to preeminence in Asia. The country's startling new wealth is making this possible, combined with the political coherence of the Chinese state in the years following Mao. This new China is still evolving; many large variables, including the ultimate role of the ruling party, are still up in the air. But China's power is clear. China today claims a geo-body commensurate with the farthest reaches of the Qing dynasty and is asserting itself aggressively on its fringes. Along the once-soft, multiethnic border connecting Southwest China and the northern tier of Southeast Asian mini-states, the Chinese state has abandoned long-practiced strategies of indirect governance and pushed state institutions and programs of Sinicization to the very border. These include militarized agricultural farms producing export commodities, especially rubber.

China's aggressive advance into the South China Sea, where several Southeast Asian countries claim maritime rights and island clusters and reefs that China also claims, is proving much more worrisome. With its newfound strength, China is now occupying some of these islets and converting them into larger ones with landfill and adding airstrips, ports, and military outposts. In the Spratly Islands, for example, these initiatives are especially alarming because, in spite of China's large presence in Southeast Asian history, it has rarely attempted to place itself physically within the region in this way.

Southeast Asian governing elites feel the pressure and, by way of a response, are balancing rather than resisting. On the one hand, they are accommodating the Chinese. In 2015, for example, all the ASEAN countries pledged to join China's new alternative to the World Bank, the Asian Infrastructure Investment Bank (AIIB). And in 2017, they hastened to attend the gala summit of China's ambitious Belt and Road initiative, which seeks to link Asia to Europe and Africa through a vast web of Chinese-built ports, industrial parks, roads, and rails. On the other hand, Southeast Asia's leaders are beefing up their ties to the West and the United States, welcoming recent U.S. economic and strategic initiatives under the Barack Obama administration and in-your-face U.S. naval exercises near China-occupied islands under the Donald Trump administration. In a case decided in 2016, the Philippines persuaded the Permanent Court of Arbitration in The Hague that China has no historical basis for its claim to waters in the West Philippine Sea.

China's new power and its growing presence in Southeast Asia empowers the region's large Chinese-descended minority, as they now form part of China's vastly expanding economy in the region. Connections to China are valuable. The stigma attached to Chinese descent that lingers in parts of Southeast Asia—in Indonesia, for example, where President Joko Widodo was slandered by his political opponents as being Chinese during the elections of 2014—may wane as the status of China itself rises. Or it may intensify if people in Southeast Asia come to feel that a rich, powerful China poses a threat and undermines national loyalties among its China-descended citizens.

Lessons of the West

Despite the remarkable rise of China in recent decades and Asia's other robust economies in Japan, South Korea, and Taiwan, Southeast Asia remains today in an age of Westernization. To be sure, in the realm of popular culture Southeast Asians savor Japanese manga and cosplay and are riveted by television dramas from South Korea. They enjoy foods and music from around the world. As always in history, they are outward looking. But when it comes to learning foreign languages, it is still English that confers status and provides entrée to the global conversation. It is still to Western universities that elite and aspiring Southeast Asians flock. (Yale, Duke, and Stanford Universities all have Singapore-based programs, alongside Wharton, INSEAD, MIT, and others.) These same universities serve as models for Southeast Asia's own burgeoning university sector, its technical institutions, and its teaching and nursing academies. And although computer technology and high-tech manufacturing are global phenomena and are fields in which many companies across Asia excel, Silicon Valley still glitters.

Moreover, Southeast Asia's nations continue to follow the Western models of government with which they began at independence, with ministries and departments and constitutions that resemble those of the West. Even the region's dictators have clothed their thuggish regimes in the language and apparatuses of democracy. Suharto arranged to have himself reelected every seven years in festive Indonesia-wide "democracy parties." Marcos held "people's referendums" in martial-law Philippines. In Thailand, power-seizing generals inevitably speak of returning the kingdom to elected governments and eventually do so. Authoritarian Singapore also holds elections regularly to relegitimize the highly disciplined and domineering People's Action Party.

Southeast Asians today are adapting what is new, attractive, and powerful in the wider world just as they once yielded to the appeal of Hinduism, Buddhism, and Islam. And just as they adopted these infusions selectively in the past—fusing what was new and exciting with what was old and comfortable—they are doing the same thing today.

Take democracy, for example. The introduction of democratic ideas and structures has altered how political power struggles occur in Southeast Asia. But it has not really altered the power structures and social hierarchies that determine who competes for power. In modern Malaysia, for example, elite Malays dominate the nation just as their ancestors dominated Malay kingdoms of old. Sultans and their titled officials and loyal chiefs have made way for the party politicians of UMNO and for prime ministers and tiers of modern elected and appointed officials (although feudal titles remain popular). Today's Malay men of prowess compete politically. And yet certain deep structures remain. Recall that all but one of Malaysia's prime ministers to date have been descendants of Malay royal families. And note that in the modern nation, as in Malay kingdoms of the past, Chinese actors play significant but subordinate roles.

The Philippines hosts a wildly popular democratic culture. Filipinos believe in elections and, despite the familiar candidate's cry of "I was cheated," honor the outcomes. They flock to the polls. But with very few exceptions, the people who run for office and win are members of an old class of prominent families whose social position and wealth date to the Spanish period. The same clans have dominated the same districts and provinces from generation to generation. Democracy has not displaced the oligarchy. It has provided a machinery for organizing the competition among its members and for legitimizing elite rule in the modern republican nation. At the same time, Philippine elections occasionally provide an opening for modern celebrities such as movie stars and athletes—huge vote-getters—to join the governing class.

Indonesia's elite Western-educated founders attempted to form a parliamentary democracy and led the new nation through its first elections. Democracy soon foundered, however, and in 1965 it was wholly overtaken by Suharto's military dictatorship. The fall of Suharto restored hopes for democracy; in fact, in the years since 1998 Indonesia has elected thousands of officials high and low, including several presidents. Despite this, many elite players under the former dictatorship continue to wield power under the new election-driven system. Political parties facilitate elite competition and serve as conduits for patronage and the spoils of office. In local elections across Indonesia, voters often favor candidates from old elite and aristocratic families. Much like the Philippines, in Indonesia, democratic elections appear to have provided a means for privileged groups to maintain their influence in a new guise. National elections in Indonesia also reveal the enduring power of Java: all but one of the country's seven presidents have been Javanese.

We can observe something similar in the region's armies and navies. From the Philippines to Thailand to Burma and Indonesia, the structure of modern militaries follows that of Western militaries, with tiers of familiar ranks and divisions of duty, i.e., infantry, ordnance, intelligence, and so on. But lurking just below the surface of the formal chain of command are structures of a personal nature that link leaders to followers and, among officers, faction to faction. (These factions often arise among graduating classes at military academies, much like fraternities.) In Southeast Asia, commanders of regional-based units and special operations foster bonds of personal loyalty with their men, making special efforts to provide for their families. These bonds endure. Patron-client ties and personal relationships like these can be activated in political crises and power struggles, pulling whole divisions one way or another. Quarreling factions in Sukarno's army led directly to his downfall in 1965; Suharto's well-cultivated following aided his rise. In 1986, General Fidel Ramos mobilized his personal ties in the Philippine military to shift support away from dictator Marcos to Marcos's rival, Corazon Aquino. The power structures of military dictatorships are riven with internal factions of this sort. In armies, too, borrowed Western structures disguise social dynamics that are deeply Southeast Asian.

Where social mobility is concerned, however, militaries and especially military dictatorships have provided new avenues for social mobility in the region. In many countries, including Indonesia and Myanmar, military officers emerged as new elites in the postindependence era. This occurred partly because military officers replaced or supplanted civilian officials in key senior functions and, significantly, because families of officers were accorded opportunities for education, travel, and experience unavailable to many ordinary people. They emerged not only as people with access to power but also as well-educated people with useful skills. Thus, to be affiliated with an officer-corps family became a distinct advantage.

Something similar is true in one-party states. In Singapore, membership in the PAP is the steppingstone to elite status in the republic. It is the same in Vietnam and Laos, where

Communist Parties still rule despite having abandoned much of communism itself.

The tension between borrowed ideas and local ones has been debated passionately from the beginning of the modern era. Southeast Asia's rising Western-educated nationalists all grappled with the problem of seizing what was best from the West without forfeiting their own hallowed beliefs and cultural identities. This led many of them to revisit their own traditions. Young Burmese radicals discovered that the teachings of modern socialism were already to be found in classical Buddhist teachings. Sukarno argued that the roots of democracy in Indonesia lay deep in the consensus-forming practices of traditional Javanese villages. Others found democracy in the Qur'an.

In more recent times, Southeast Asian leaders wishing to restrain unfettered popular democracy have also appealed to tradition. Sukarno did exactly that when he suppressed his new country's quarreling political parties in favor of "Guided Democracy." Mahathir Mohamad, the authoritarian prime minister of Malaysia from 1982 to 2003, appealed to "Asian Values." In a similar vein, Singapore's founder Lee Kuan Yew defended his predilection for elite-led authoritarianism and his critique of Western individualism in Confucian terms. And what is "Thai democracy"? In Thailand, power-seizing generals and their elite civil-society supporters in recent years have overthrown popularly elected civilian governments on the grounds that they violated Thai values honoring religion, monarchy, and the nation.

Religious identities

Religion is another arena where resistance to the West's influence is strong. Flourishing movements among Southeast Asian Buddhists and Muslims emphasize reasserting religious values in the face of the highly individualistic values of the West. This is especially strong among the region's Muslims, who make up

37 percent of the population. Keep in mind that, today, virtually all Muslim young people yearn to use computers and high-tech smartphones. They are avid consumers of Western culture in the forms of music, films, and television shows. In these ways they are thoroughly modern. But they are also emphatically Muslim.

Throughout Muslim Southeast Asia today, mosques are full; young people and their elders regularly gather to study and pray; people increasingly use Arabic salutations in social encounters and public events; Muslim self-improvement books, videos, and television shows proliferate; and Muslim women wear head scarves and appropriately modest clothing in accordance with conservative practices. (For the youth, blue jeans are often part of the ensemble.) These phenomena emphasize the positive identity of Islam.

Embedded within this larger phenomenon are social and ideological movements that are politically assertive, including political parties in Malaysia and Indonesia that campaign for making the laws of Islam (Sharia) the laws of the land. In a handful of provinces they have succeeded, but by and large they have not. The debate remains a lively one. Meanwhile, national governments have stepped up their support for Islam in the realms of education and mosque building and in facilitating the Hajj. In Malaysia especially, the ruling party has increasingly adopted the mantle of Islam as part of the country's Malay identity.

At the same time, more extreme Muslim subcultures have also penetrated Southeast Asia, recruiting small numbers into exclusionist cults and jihadist movements associated with global assaults aimed at the West, such as al-Qaeda and ISIS (Islamic State). Extremists have been identified in Malaysia, Indonesia, and the southern Philippines. In Indonesia sporadic terrorist attacks have occurred, including the infamous Bali bombings of 2001 and others, more recently, in Jakarta. This radical fringe does not speak for the vast majority. Still, it puts the region's Muslims on edge and acts as an alarm factor for Christian minorities, who in today's Malaysia and Indonesia are already inclined to feel beleaguered in the face of an assertive Islam. An unfortunate consequence of this has been Muslim-Christian violence in several places in Indonesia.

Across the mainland, Buddhism remains the religious discourse through which most Thais, Burmese, Lao, and Cambodians understand and interpret the contemporary world. This can take multiple forms, from the purely contemplative to the politically engaged. Buddhism is invoked with respect to every issue, from poverty, crime, and gender to kingship and democracy. New sects flourish. In places, Buddhism is highly politicized, especially in Myanmar, where Buddhists are an empowered majority. As noted, longstanding tensions and rivalries between Buddhists and Muslims in some areas lie behind recent bloody outbursts and the flow of Muslim refugees abroad.

Meanwhile, Christianity is growing in Southeast Asia. Significant populations of Christians have been present in the region for a long time in the Philippines, Vietnam, East Timor, and parts of eastern Indonesia. Christian missionaries during the high colonial period created further pockets of Christians in Burma and Indonesia. In the years since independence, Catholicism has advanced among the region's ethnic Chinese populations in Indonesia and elsewhere, and Protestant sects have advanced generally, especially Pentecostal and evangelical denominations that have evangelized the region's now-exposed hill peoples and restless urbanites in places like Singapore. Today, a quarter of all Southeast Asians are Christian.

Yet, even as world-religion identities grow stronger in Southeast Asia, the region's cultures of fusion and tolerance survive. In one telling example, two thousand-year-old Hindu temples recently unearthed on the campus of the Islamic University of Indonesia will not be destroyed or covered up but will instead be displayed prominently on the Muslim campus. As for Southeast Asia's primordial spirits, they live on comfortably embedded within the everyday spiritual habits of millions of the region's Buddhists, Muslims, and Christians. Spirits rarely make the news but, in 2015, they did so when the deputy chief minister of Sabah, Malaysia, blamed a deadly earthquake on foreign tourists who had stripped naked on Mount Kinabalu and disturbed the local spirits. To appease them, rituals were duly held.

A beleaguered habitat

Visitors to Southeast Asia today from outside the region arrive at swanky international airports in or near a capital city and many will not stray far from these megacities—Bangkok, Singapore, Manila, Jakarta—and their five-star hotels, modern office buildings, fashionable restaurants, and chic shopping malls or from well-traveled tourist pathways that lead to museums, monuments, and beaches. Yet even privileged travelers cannot altogether escape the profound environmental forces that impact ordinary Southeast Asians.

The human habitat of today's Southeast Asia has been shaped by the region's accelerating participation in global trade, leading growing numbers of people to press into the region's forests, wetlands, and hills to reap subsistence and profits from the land. Much of the region's old-growth forest has succumbed to loggers and agribusiness companies and, in places, to needy farmers. Some of the land has been converted into industrial tree plantations and other monocultures, but much has simply been degraded. Silted rivers and downstream floods are other common consequences of this transformation, along with declining biodiversity and animal habitat and the loss of the climate-regulating benefits of forests.

Efforts to convert remaining forests in Kalimantan and Sumatra to oil palm and paper-wood plantations are so aggressive that companies induce massive fires to clear the land. Smoke from these fires rolls across the earth, creating sickening fumes in Jakarta, Singapore, Kuala Lumpur, and southern Thailand. People wear face masks in defense. Otherwise, it is the exhaust from the surging numbers of cars, trucks, buses, and motorbikes that dirties the air of the region's cities. Asthma, bronchitis, and lung disease plague millions of urbanites. The water is not clean either, as unchecked human and industrial waste, not to mention simple trash, flows into the rivers, lakes, bays, and city canals. In Southeast Asia the rule has become bottled water only, please.

Southeast Asians are justly alarmed about this. Activists are vocal, and conscientious politicians are enacting sensible laws. Forest rangers and air-quality inspectors are at work. Indeed, ASEAN task forces, scientists, technocrats, ministers, government officials, and nongovernmental organizations (NGOs) are urgently trying to turn the tide. They are succeeding here and there. But by and large they are no match for the huge global forces driving the world's economy or for the powerful local interests in Southeast Asia who have much to gain from their failure. The hard truth is that the assault on Southeast Asia's environment continues largely unabated today.

The situation is scarcely different in China or India or much of the developing world. The impact of globalization, climate change, and the scramble for the earth's resources is universal. As a habitat for humans and other living things, Southeast Asia is inextricably part of these larger forces. Its fate is also the fate of the earth.

References

Chapter 2: Kingdoms

The essential point about power arising from control of people is emphasized by Anthony Reid in *Southeast Asia in the Age of Commerce, 1450–1680*, vol. 1, *The Land below the Winds* (New Haven, CT: Yale University Press, 1988). The description of Southeast Asian warfare and of early-modern Southeast Asian commerce also largely follows Reid, *Southeast Asia in the Age of Commerce, 1450–1680*, vol. 1, *The Land below the Winds*, and vol. 2, *Expansion and Crisis*.

For mandalas, see Stanley J. Tambiah, "The Galactic Polity in Southeast Asia," *Hau: Journal of Ethnographic Theory* 3.3 (2013): 503–534; and O. W. Wolters, *History, Culture, and Region in Southeast Asian Perspectives* (Ithaca, NY: Cornell Southeast Asia Program, 1999). Wolters introduced the term "men of prowess."

For patron-client ties, a good place to begin is James C. Scott, "Patron-Client Politics and Political Change in Southeast Asia," *The American Political Science Review* 66.1 (1972): 91–113.

The idea that Southeast Asians chose to live in inaccessible uplands to be free, is presented in James C. Scott, *The Art of Not Being Governed: An Anarchist History of Upland Southeast Asia* (New Haven, CT: Yale University Press, 2010).

The term "mystic synthesis," to describe Java's Hindu-Buddhist-Islamic ways, comes from M. C. Ricklefs, *Mystic Synthesis in Java: A History of Islamization from the Fourteenth to the Early Nineteenth Centuries* (Norwalk, CT: EastBridge Signature Books, 2006).

Chapter 3: Colonies

Conrad quotation is from Joseph Conrad, *Outcast of the Islands* (London: J. M. Dent, 1949), 57.

Swettenham quotation is from Frank Swettenham, *British Malaya: An Account of the Origin and Progress of British Influence in Malaya* (London: John Lane, 1907), 345.

Chapter 4: Nations

Kipling quotation is from Rudyard Kipling, "Mandalay," in *Barrack-Room Ballads and Other Verses* (London: Methuen, 1892).

On nations as geo-bodies, see Thongchai Winichakul, *Siam Mapped: A History of the Geo-body of a Nation* (Honolulu: University of Hawaii Press, 1994).

Chapter 5: The past is in the present

On Southeast Asian democracy, see, inter alia, Edward Aspinall, "The Surprising Democratic Behemoth: Indonesia in Comparative Asian Perspective," *Journal of Asian Studies* 74.4 (2015): 889–902; and Mark R. Thompson, "Democracy with Asian Characteristics," *Journal of Asian Studies* 74.4 (2015): 875–887.

On Thailand's Muslim south, see Michael Montesano and Patrick Jory, eds., *Thai South and Malay North: Ethnic Interactions on a Plural Peninsula* (Singapore: National University of Singapore Press, 2008).

On Sulu Sea issues, see Katrina Navallo, "Filipino Migrants in Sabah: Marginalized Citizens in the Midst of Interstate Disputes," Academia.edu, 2015.

On the fate of the hills, see Jefferson Fox, Yayoi Fujita, Dimbab Ngidang, et al. "Policies, Political-Economy and Swidden in Southeast Asia," *Human Ecology* 37.3 (2009): 305–322.

Further reading

Chapter 1: What is Southeast Asia?

Beeson, Mark, ed. *Contemporary Southeast Asia*. London: Palgrave Macmillan, 2009. See especially Greg Felker, "The Political Economy of Southeast Asia," 46–73.

Dayley, Robert, and Clark D. Neher. *Southeast Asia in the New International Arena*. Boulder, CO: Westview, 2013.

Duncan, Christopher R. *Civilizing the Margins: Southeast Asian Government Policies for the Development of Minorities*. Ithaca, NY: Cornell University Press, 2004.

Jones, Gavin W. "The Population of Southeast Asia," Asia Research Institute, Working Paper 196. Singapore: National University of Singapore, 2013.

Robison, Richard, ed. *Routledge Handbook of Southeast Asian Politics*. London: Routledge, 2014. See especially Jeffrey A. Winters, "Oligarchs and Oligarchy in Southeast Asia," 53–67.

Scott, James C. *The Art of Not Being Governed: An Anarchist History of Southeast Asia*. New Haven, CT: Yale University Press, 2010.

Chapter 2: Kingdoms

Andaya, Barbara Watson, and Leonard Y. Andaya. *A History of Early Modern Southeast Asia*. Cambridge, UK: Cambridge University Press, 2015.

Coedès, George. *The Indianized States of Southeast Asia*. Translated by Susan Cowing. Honolulu: Hawaii East-West Center Press, 1968.

Lieberman, Victor. *Strange Parallels: Southeast Asia in Global Context, c800–1830*. 2 vols. Cambridge, UK: Cambridge University Press, 2003–2009.

Reid, Anthony. *Southeast Asia in the Age of Commerce*. 2 vols. New Haven, CT: Yale University Press, 1988–1993.

Tarling, Nicholas, ed. *The Cambridge History of Southeast Asia: From Early Times to c1500*. Vol. 1. Cambridge, UK: Cambridge University Press, 1999.

Wolters, O. W. *History, Culture, and Region in Southeast Asian Perspectives*. Ithaca, NY: Cornell University Southeast Asia Program, 1999.

Woodside, Alexander. *Vietnam and the Chinese Model: A Comparative Study of Nguyen and Ch'ing Government in the First Half of the Nineteenth Century*. Cambridge, MA: Harvard University Press, 1971.

Chapter 3: Colonies

Brocheux, Pierre, and Daniel Hémery. *Indochina: An Ambiguous Colonization, 1858–1954*. Berkeley: University of California Press, 2009.

Conrad, Joseph. *An Outcast of the Islands*. 1896. Reprint, Cambridge, UK: Cambridge University Press, 2016.

Conrad, Joseph. *Lord Jim*. 1900. Reprint, Cambridge, UK: Cambridge University Press, 2011.

Couperus, Louis. *The Hidden Force*. 1900. Translated by Alexander Texeira de Mattos. Amherst: University of Massachusetts Press, 1985.

Duras, Marguerite. *The Lover*. Translated by Barbara Bray. New York: Pantheon Books, 1985.

Cribb, Robert, ed. *The Late Colonial State in Indonesia: Political and Economic Foundations of the Netherlands Indies, 1880–1942*. Leiden, The Netherlands: KITLV Press, 1994.

Furnivall, J. S. *Netherlands India: A Study of a Plural Economy*. Cambridge, UK: Cambridge University Press, 1944.

McCoy, Alfred W. *Policing America's Empire: The United States, the Philippines, and the Rise of the Surveillance State*. Part 1. Madison: University of Wisconsin Press, 2009.

Orwell, George. *Burmese Days*. 1934. Reprint, London: Penguin, 2014.

Owen, Norman G. *Prosperity without Progress: Manila Hemp and Material Life in the Colonial Philippines*. Berkeley: University of California Press, 1984.

Phelan, John Leddy. *The Hispanization of the Philippines: Spanish Aims and Filipino Responses, 1565–1700*. Madison: University of Wisconsin Press, 1959.

Reid, Anthony, ed. *Sojourners and Settlers: Histories of Southeast Asia and the Chinese*. Sydney: Allen & Unwin, 1996.

Ricklefs, M. C., Bruce Lockhart, Albert Lau, Portia Reyes, and Maitrii Aung-Thwin. *A New History of Southeast Asia*. Basingstoke, UK: Palgrave Macmillan, 2010.

Tagliacozzo, Eric. *Secret Trades, Porous Borders: Smuggling and States along a Southeast Asian Frontier, 1865–1915*. New Haven, CT: Yale University Press, 2005.

Thongchai Winichakul. *Siam Mapped: A History of the Geo-body of a Nation*. Honolulu: University of Hawaii Press, 1994.

Chapter 4: Nations

Anderson, Benedict R. O'Gorman. *Imagined Communities: Reflections on the Origin and Spread of Nationalism*. London: Verso, 2006.

Bradley, Mark Philip. *Vietnam at War*. Oxford: Oxford University Press, 2009.

Chandler, David P. *The Tragedy of Cambodian History: Politics, War, and Revolution since 1945*. New Haven, CT: Yale University Press, 1991.

Edwards, Penny. *Cambodge: The Cultivation of a Nation, 1860–1945*. Honolulu: University of Hawaii Press, 2007.

Elson, Robert E. *The Idea of Indonesia: A History*. Cambridge, UK: Cambridge University Press, 2008.

Evans, Grant. *A Short History of Laos: The Land in Between*. Chiang Mai, Thailand: Silkworm Books, 2002.

Kahin, George McTurnan. *Nationalism and Revolution in Indonesia*. Ithaca, NY: Cornell University Press, 1952.

McCoy, Alfred W., ed. *Southeast Asia under Japanese Occupation*. New Haven, CT: Yale University Southeast Asia Studies, 1980.

Marr, David. *Vietnamese Anticolonialism, 1885–1925*. Berkeley: University of California Press, 1971.

Robinson, Geoffrey. *The Dark Side of Paradise: Political Violence on Bali*. Ithaca, NY: Cornell University Press, 1995.

Shiraishi, Takashi. *An Age in Motion: Popular Radicalism in Java, 1912–1926*. Ithaca, NY: Cornell University Press, 1990.

Taylor, Robert H. *The State in Myanmar*. Honolulu: University of Hawaii Press, 2009.

Zinoman, Peter. *The Colonial Bastille: The History of Imprisonment in Vietnam, 1862–1940*. Berkeley: University of California Press, 2001.

Chapter 5: The past is in the present

Anderson, Benedict R. O'Gorman. *The Spectre of Comparisons: Nationalism, Southeast Asia, and the World*. Manila: Ateneo de Manila University Press, 2004.

Hefner, Robert W. *Civil Islam: Muslims and Democratization in Indonesia*. Princeton, NJ: Princeton University Press, 2000.

Ricklefs, M. C. *Islamization and Its Opponents in Java, c1300 to the Present*. Honolulu: University of Hawaii Press, 2012.

Schober, Juliane. *Modern Buddhist Conjunctures in Myanmar: Cultural Narratives, Colonial Legacies, and Civil Society*. Honolulu: University of Hawaii Press, 2011.

Sidel, John T. *Capital, Coercion, and Crime: Bossism in the Philippines*. Stanford, CA: Stanford University Press, 1999.

Good feature writing about current affairs in Southeast Asia can be found on the *Wall Street Journal*, *New York Times*, and BBC websites alongside those of many regional newspapers and article aggregators / new portals, e.g., the Philippines-based Rappler and the Australia National University–based *New Mandala*. Economic data and reports on contemporary issues, such as poverty, human trafficking, the environment, etc., can be found on several United Nations websites, such as the United Nations High Commissioner for Refugees (UNHCR), United Nations Development Programme (UNDP), United Nations Environment Programme (UNEP), United Nations Children's Fund (UNICEF), United Nations Economic and Social Commission for Asia and the Pacific (ESCAP), and UN News Centre; see also the World Bank, Asian Development Bank (ADB), Association of Southeast Asian Nations (ASEAN), World Resources Institute (WRI), Amnesty International, and World Wildlife Fund (WWF). Useful academic journals include *Contemporary Southeast Asia*, *Asian Survey*, *Sojourns*, and the *Journal of Southeast Asian Studies*.

Index

Southeast Asia